WAS IT WORTH IT

Mill Farm Salt Spring Island

Bruce R.E. Williams

ISBN: 1523950951
ISBN 13: 9781523950959

CONTENTS

MILL FARM

In the beginning, I had absolutely no idea that there was a possibility we could lose the court case that was filed against us because I had never signed the form to redevelop our communal land. Our lawyer said that all ten members of the Mill Farm Cooperative had to agree to anything that would happen to the land. Our lawyer registered the Mill Farm as a one-tenth undivided interest in the aforementioned lands, which was comprised of 160 acres on the registered title at the Land Title and Survey Authority office in Victoria, British Columbia.

After we were served the court documents to appear before a judge, I came home one day, and my wife said, "I wonder what would have happened if we had signed that agreement?" I could tell that she was at her breaking point as her lips tightened like a dried-up prune. Before we left for Mexico, she looked like a bone rack from riding her bike constantly up and down the mountain. The stress of our situation was written all over her body like rivulets of blackened sinew stretched beyond repair, running the length of her muscled legs.

My mind goes back to why I ever made the decision to not sign those papers that hammer white survey stakes into the earth. The decision cost my family and good friends $250,000, which each shareholder technically could have made if I'd signed those papers. My decision made me the bad guy to everyone who was a partner in the Mill Farm and to the local government that approved the subdivision without any environmental studies whatsoever. I knew, deep down, that even my wife and family thought I was crazy and out of my mind. How could I not sign those papers that would have made our house and my son's house legal entities in the middle of the sacred grove of the old-growth fir forest?

I really believe in karma above all. I had done a lot of things in my life but always made a promise to myself never to place survey stakes into the ground, thus subdividing any piece of our Mother Earth. That was the main reason I bought my share in the Mill Farm Cooperative in what was supposed to be a communal living situation.

The consequences of my nightmare have led me to share my trials and tribulations with others so they don't have to go through the same hell that our family had to endure—a result of the hate and greed that ran through human beings with only one thought in their mind: to succeed at Mother Nature's expense.

One of the reasons the Mill Farm Cooperative became an international story was that the Island Trust accepted a signature from an unregistered owner that turned our fondest dream into a nightmare from hell. This experience dragged all my faith in friendship down to the ocean depths, choking it like a fish out of water gasping for its last breath. My strong belief that my partners had integrity had been shattered, and my self-respect as well as my dignity went out the window like a spirit in the night.

The Mill Farm came up as an estate sale in 1981. It went on the auction block so that the highest bidder would own the rights for 160 acres of prime, old-growth fir with old homestead buildings and a water wheel built on it. You guessed right! We were going up against the loggers to buy this piece of incredible land to save it from logging. Our dream was to form a cooperative with an alternative lifestyle as the focal point.

The main reason we all got to be owners of the Mill Farm was due to a wonderful woman who got her family's inheritance. In the beginning, we had no idea how lucky we were going to be because of a mistake made in the final amount on the check. It was decided that we would put in an offer of $250,000 to the estate of the Mill Farm. When our benefactor wrote out the check, she made a slip of the pen. It was one of the best mistakes of her life, and she accidentally wrote it out for $255,000. The loggers wrote theirs out for $250,000. The Mill Farm estate was sold to the highest bid, which was the Mill Farm Cooperative. We had "accidentally" fulfilled our dream. We all felt, at the time, that it was a very favorable omen! Little did we know that the incorrect check was the first mistake in a long line of heartaches, broken dreams, disappointments, and quite a few gray hairs for all of those involved in the venture.

In the beginning, we had meetings every day. Everyone was very enthusiastic to figure out the best way to accomplish our dreams. This wasn't as easy as you might think. One of the main concerns was schooling for the children, as there were approximately sixteen children of school age. The road was also very rutted with huge potholes. Not one person had a vehicle in those days that could make the eight-mile journey on a regular basis. We thought because there were enough children, we would be able to get money from the government to build our own school. After all, we had two of the local schoolteachers in our cooperative. During those early meetings, we had huge discussions on where the outhouse would be built and whether or not it would be a composting one. We even argued about who would clean it out. We didn't miss much at those early meetings.

Imagine twelve people's dreams being intertwined, while at the same time numerous children with long dresses and hair flowing in the breeze were running around, having the time of their lives. It was absolutely fantastic. Especially, when the heiress's ex came down from the north to build a sweat lodge big enough for all of us to sit in. The idea was to cleanse our spirits to help us live among these giant old-growth fir trees that encircled us and towered above us, like angels looking over our families.

At the meetings, it was decided that people could buy a share of the Mill Farm for one dollar down, and payments made on a monthly basis on a 12 percent interest scale. Each share would cost $25,500. Before any person could buy a share, he had to be approved by the group. At the onset there were even honorary members who had voting rights. On the title, we were registered as *Tenants in Common* with a one-tenth undivided interest in the 160-acre parcel. We were led to believe that this would protect the land because all ten people would have to approve any major development, such as logging, subdivision, roads, and septic infrastructure. The very essence of the original agreement was to have as little impact as possible on the land, including no survey stakes period, and to live harmoniously with the environment in perpetuity.

The old farm site consisted of a derelict barn, complete with a roof that had caved in many winters ago. The roof was no longer strong enough to carry the burden of the snow's weight, and there was a burned-out old house and a broken-down water wheel. In the early days, before a lot of the mountain was logged, there was plenty of water to run the wheel. There were two sets of stories about the wheel. Some old-timers say it was used to saw lumber, while others say it was used to grind flour and as a sharpening stone. When I first saw the wheel in the mid-1970s, it was still pretty intact, and there was no evidence of a sawmill site. You would need a big area for a sawmill site. The water wheel also wasn't in an area where you could move logs around. I wonder to this day if it could have been used to create power to run one of those old Ono 12 volt generators.

In those days, the only access was by boat, arriving at Musgrave Landing. The homestead had definitely seen better days. In the 1960s and 1970s, people squatted all over the mountain and stayed in the old house on the Mill Farm. There was even a piano in it at the time. The story goes that some of the locals got tired of the squatters living there and burned the old house down. All that was left of the original house were the charred remains of the homesteaders' labor of love. Coals lay lifeless, burned black in the old root cellar below the house, outlined by blackened stones used as the foundation. The fire that swept through the place also burned a few trees in the orchard. Their charred remnants solemnly stood guard over the once grand estate. The scene always sends my imagination whirling. How amazing it would have been to be living on the Mill Farm at that time. There was a thriving, self-sufficient community of twenty-nine families spread out over the mountain in the 1920s and 1930s. At that time, there was even a post office on the Mill Farm, which was moved to another location on the mountain and became a local caretaker's home.

After the farm was purchased, we had a lot of worker bees among us. The first thing we did was build a fence around a garden site. Each share had a spot in the garden. In no time the bare land flourished, and the vegetables and the beauty of the flowers enriched the old farmstead. Another project was to tear down the old, broken-down roof of the barn, replacing it with a new roof.

The dreams that we had for the back meadow started to unfold when we cleared two acres of land on a southwest-facing slope, while to the north was a glorious stand of old-growth fir trees. We even hired an excavator to dig out a huge hole where there was evidence of a spring, in order to make a pond. The dirt from the pond was spread out over the meadow to create a spot for a volleyball court. Many of us from the south end of Salt Spring Island played volleyball, and every year we would go to a different island that would host a volleyball tournament. Yes, the rumors you heard about us playing naked were true. There were always a few free spirits who would shed it all. These tournaments also would fall during harvest season, when people would always be proud of their summers endeavors and want to share the experience with whoever wanted to try out their crops of green treats. It was always fun to see who produced the best crop of weed.

In those days, Stoll Lake was a nude beach. All of the locals would cool off in the lake on hot summer days. They would just stop during their busy day, strip off their clothes, and jump into the lake. There were a few people who were lying around tanning; after drying off that way, they would go. I will never forget the day that an off-island cyclist was coming around the corner at Stoll Lake, and after seeing some of our local women topless, he rode right off the road into the blackberry bushes. I lived in a home we built above Stoll Lake before buying into the Mill Farm Cooperative.

After the purchase of the Mill Farm, we had a potluck supreme, all home-baked goods and most of the food was vegetarian dishes. The women wore long velour dresses and the children ran through the meadow with long tresses blowing in their wake. There was even a tepee set up at the old farm site, which looked lovely with its twelve poles spiraling toward the heavens.

There were pieces of land that became common areas; the "Sacred Grove" was the most incredible, with a circle of old-growth firs sheltering a small clearing. These gigantic trees were so tall that they seemed to shoot up all the way to the cosmos. Their majesty was at its most splendid around sunset. The opulence was almost blinding as the sun streamed in through needles, branches, and moss. It was a magnificent spectrum that consisted of a glorious palate of orange, green, and brown, painting a most delightful picture.

The old-timers say that the people who owned it were Rosicrucian and had candlelight ceremonies in the Sacred Grove.

The Mill Farm was one of the only pieces of land that wasn't logged in those days, which led me to believe that the first people who owned it had a real connection to the land. We found phantom orchids growing in the Sacred Grove one year; apparently they can stay dormant for many years before they come out.

The back meadow was also chosen as a common area where there would be a pond and volleyball court built there one day. The other main piece of common land was the Mill Farm site itself. Some people intended to have a commune-type living situation, including a large building that housed a communal kitchen, workshop, and school. No, this wasn't taking place in the '60s; we were a group of people from the '60s still trying to live out their dream in 1981. Some people got ticked off right away because they had their hearts set on certain areas where they wanted to build their houses. Some of these became common areas, so they couldn't choose them as homesites. They couldn't see themselves anywhere else on the 160 acres and decided not to buy a share. There were some major heated arguments over this in the beginning, and many hurt feelings.

Other sites that were chosen had views that would make your heart soar into the heavens because of their magnificent beauty. Oceans, straits, bays, and visual faults where the earth protruded on Vancouver Island like a tectonic plate gone wild encircled these incredible sites. The fast-rushing currents of Samsun Narrows meandered below us, making a seaway for tugs and log booms along with pleasure crafts. From our deck sometimes we would witness a tug pulling a barge full of lumber. One time we saw a small boat pull up behind the barge close enough for someone to jump on the back of it and cut the bindings that held the lumber secure. Before you knew it, the lumber was falling into the fast-moving waters of the strait. These pieces of lumber would end up in the small bays, to be picked up later for building someone's dream home. There was no way in the world that the tugboat crew could do anything but keep going straight in order to keep the tug and barge on course.

We took notes during those meetings, writing down the bylaws regarding things like how many times the outhouse would be emptied and how to go about choosing a housing site, which could only have one house and a guest house built on it. The haggling started when shareholders began trying to figure out the Mill Farm Constitution. Most members and honorary members were hippies from the '60s who never fulfilled the dream of that era of younger people who wanted to live in the past in a simpler time.

One guy took acid and spent the day scanning the land, which went from seven hundred to eighteen hundred feet above sea level, until he had the right alignment with the cosmos, and then chose his site. Once you chose a building site, the whole group had to approve it. The first few who chose their building sites had it easy because everyone was there to approve their sites. Natural landmarks marked the sites, such as trees and boulders. Most sites were between one and three acres in size and were accessible by old trails. People labored happily on their building sites, moving stones and planning out their dream homes.

Some people's ideals changed rather quickly, and many didn't last a full year when they realized that the previous one dollar down was a lot easier to come up with than having to pay the monthly payment. They couldn't afford two lives, so they returned their shares to our benefactor. A lot of the shareholders started realizing the hardship of living off the land and tried to drive over the hill to work in town. The commute was a killer, but the mortgage had to be paid. Many of the shareholders ended up renting or buying in town. They hadn't thought about how inconvenient it would be living so far from work, shops, gas stations, and the local swimming lakes. The notion of homeschooling had apparently dissipated, and being near schools became an important issue for some.

AFTER LUNCH

I always wanted to buy into the Mill Farm in a big way, but my partner at the time definitely didn't want to and was very much against it. One day I went home to have lunch with my wife and daughter. After lunch we put our daughter down for her nap. My wife came out of the bedroom with a packed bag and said she was leaving and didn't want me to follow her. I never saw this coming until it blindsided me like a cyclone, all after we had quietly ate our lunch. There was no warning, nothing; she just evaporated into thin air, leaving me a single dad with two children. All that was on my mind was what I would tell our son when he got home from school and asked, "Where is Mom?"

Things in my life soon changed quickly, especially after I learned that our bank account was dry and a credit card we had together was up to the maximum limit. Many of the cancelled checks were made out to the local cocaine dealer. I was right in the middle of designing and making a drop-in skylight system, which I registered and made into a limited company. I had orders, and we were making them in my shop out of the back of our house. I realized the first night after she left that I didn't know what to do. I was sitting in a closet with a gun stuck in my mouth, ready to pull the trigger. Thank goodness I still had a sense of the situation and never pulled the trigger.

I made the decision that night to sell my skylight system to another company in Vancouver. One of the first things I did afterward was go over there and sell them the design and the limited company. The company that I sold it to was also designing the first drop skylight, but the problem with theirs was they were made out of vinyl and the ultraviolet rays destroyed them. My "Star Lights" system had an aluminum cover on them to solve this problem, and in fact, some of them are still in houses today on Salt Spring Island.

In the 1960s, I was always the babysitter for all my friends doing LSD (acid). I learned a lot about the trip by watching them. We had a friend that wasn't so lucky and jumped out of a twenty-story building when a knock came at the door. The only thing that we could come up with was that he might have thought the knock on the door was the police. We called them narcs in those days, which were undercover cops pretending to be hip.

I always figured if the day came that I ever needed to use acid, I would use it as a tool. So I got a babysitter and asked a friend of mine to get me some LSD, which he did, and bless him, he stayed with me while I tripped out. What it did was speed things up in my mind and gave me a better understanding of what I had to do. Being a single parent was a full-time job, coupled with the fact that I was taking care of my business, so I had to put the idea of buying the Mill Farm on hold. After some time, we sold our family home and split the money.

SCHOOL BUS

With part of my money, I bought a Sunday school's bus that still had all the seats in it. I fixed it up with enough beds to sleep nine and hit the road with some friends during the music festivals. We sold burritos at the old Courtney Fair, Barnes Creek, Edmonton, and Vancouver Music Festivals. We even did a country music festival in Brooks, Alberta, and at the Williams Lake Rodeo. I had the time of my life at these fairs. It was so much fun. I could go on and on talking about our adventures doing those old fairs, but I had better get back to the story at hand.

When I came back to Salt Spring that fall after doing these fairs, I drove my bus over the mountain to squat on a piece of land above the Mill Farm. This ended up being one of the scariest things that ever happened to me. I drove through the Laundry Farm and proceeded up a steep trail to the north of their place. The trail was level at first, but then it got steeper. I got halfway up this steep hill and then something broke on the drive train of the bus, and it started freewheeling down the mountain. I stomped on the brake, it went to the floor, and I pushed so hard I broke the driver's seat bracket. I had to grab onto the steering wheel hard to keep myself from falling backward. I knew I had to act fast and do something. Near the bottom of the hill was another trail crossing the one I was on, so when I got close to it, I cranked the wheel hard. The bus smashed into a rock and came to a dead stop and just about flipped over on its side. After coming to a sudden stop when I hit the rock, the impact was so hard that all of the cupboards, shelves, and stuff I built was just a pile on the floor about two feet deep.

I couldn't deal with it at that moment and just went to sleep. The next day a logger that was logging the Laundry Farm kindly pulled my bus up the hill with his Caterpillar. I directed him to a site above the Mill Farm, high up the mountain with a great view. My dream was always to buy a share in the Mill Farm. I always joined the meetings in the beginning and talked to all the worker bees.

YELAPA

I left my bus up on the mountain and went to Mexico for the winter. It was the first time I went to Yelapa. What an amazing place it was! No roads or electricity was high on my list of likes, at least in this young man's mind. I was supposed to meet a friend in Belize, but really got caught up with the wonderful people in Yelapa.

When I got off the *Sarape*, the boat that brought me to Yelapa from Puerto Vallarta, I got into an old dugout wooden canoe. Standing at the back of the canoe was a young man with a large paddle, navigating it to the small beach in the Pueblo. As soon as I got on the beach, a couple—along with a local—came up to me and said that they had to go back to the States because of a family issue. They told me that they rented a house from this man; there were still three weeks left on the rental contract and they were willing to let me take over.

When we went to look at the house, we crossed a small creek where women were washing their clothes. The house was alone on a hillside overlooking the creek. When I went in, I saw a small but clean kitchen with a sitting room and a ladder that went to a loft above the sitting room. Off the back was a lean-to that was the bathroom. I liked it a lot and agreed to take it for the remaining time.

I went back down to the beach to get my bag and headed back up to my new digs. When I went in the door, it was as we had left it moments before. I went up the ladder to the loft, which had a swinging bed, covered with a mosquito net, suspended from the ceiling. The reason for this was because there were a lot of scorpions in Yelapa. The suspended bed stopped them from crawling up the bed legs, and the net stopped them from dropping on you from a roof made out of palm tree branches. When I went back down the ladder, I noticed a small jar on the table with one rose in it. I never heard anyone come in or leave the place, and a big question mark started forming in my mind. How did that glass jar and fresh rose get there on that table?

I went down to the beach, which had many local restaurants and served fresh foods from the Pueblo along with fresh fish from the sea. There was a group of people sitting together who invited me to sit down. I'm still friends with some of these people from those days. They were playing a game where you could be anyone you wanted to be in Gwavunah, an imaginary place where the group had control. It was so much fun. One guy wanted to be a car salesman in a place that had no roads. Another was a woman who was a veterinarian and wanted to be princess of the imaginary country. We really had a lot of fun sitting on the beach playing this game. As we sat there, an old guy came riding down the beach on a white horse and behind him was tethered another white horse loaded down with bulging bags. I soon learned that those were the crops of marijuana harvested from the fields in the mountains.

One moment I even told the group about my experience renting the house. Some of them said the family crisis was just an excuse so the Americans could leave because the wife was afraid and thought there was a spirit in the house. Then a woman walked up and asked if anyone knew a place to rent because she didn't like her place. There weren't many places to rent at that time, and one of the main places for rent was an old *palapa* that had a huge platform built down the middle. It was separated with mosquito nets and each space was rented out for five dollars per night. She wasn't happy with this arrangement and was looking for something else. A man covered in tattoos said that I had a place, and that there was a cot in the sitting room. So we made a deal and off we went to show her my space.

The first morning, she was very upset and afraid. She said she felt like there was a spirit in the house. When she went into the kitchen, she felt an energy all around her that made her feel quizzical—in other words the hair on the back of her neck stood on end. After some more experiences like that, she left after three days. She was supposed to spend a week in Yelapa but left on the boat to Puerto Vallarta. The tattooed man just laughed when I told him the whole story. She was there waiting for the boat, and I told her story about the spirit and why she was leaving out of fear. It seemed like a recurring experience in those times. The day before, the tattooed man had come down and was so excited that he had rented his *palapa* above the village.

Then he laughed and said, "Let's see if I have to stay somewhere else tonight, instead of my place." It was apparently a huge part of the daily entertainment there, of which I soon became aware. He said not once did the people actually stay a night in his place, and it was how he made his money to sit on the beach and drink beer. He would rent his quaint little *palapa* to anyone getting off the boat looking for a place. He would take the people to his place, show them around, make sure he had the money in his hand, and then come back down to the beach. When I first witnessed this, I was amazed by what went on. When he got back to the beach, everyone would guess how long it would take for the people to come back down and tell their story. He had only come back for an hour when his renters came down to the beach, carrying their bags. As soon as they got there, the man he rented to said that they didn't want to stay there and wanted their money back. The tattooed man said no and mentioned that it was a deal that they paid for.

The man responded, "There is no way we can stay with that snake in the house!" The snake in question lived in the rafters of the *palapa,* and it would all of a sudden drop down from its perch above, landing on the table. This went on all the time and the tattooed man afterward would go back to stay in his place. He never even had to rent a place for the night because no one ever ended up staying a whole night.

When I got up the next day, I went down the ladder from my loft to make breakfast. I made a nice little breakfast, left the dishes, went back up the ladder to make my bed, and got ready for the beach. I could not believe what I witnessed: my bed was already made. I know for a fact that I never made it, and I never heard a sound. I got ready for the beach and went down the ladder. Now I was starting to wonder big-time, my dishes were already done, all nicely cleaned up and put away.

Little could I ever imagine what was in store for me in the coming days. The next day, I lay in my swinging bed and felt energy near me. I opened my eyes and saw my first spirit, sitting there all calm at the foot of my bed. He was wearing a hat and looked very old and wrinkled; before I knew it, he was gone in a flash.

I started feeling something different happening with me after this. One example was how I would go up the river every morning to a waterfall and have my bath. A song started coming out of me as I drummed on one of the rocks. I stopped drinking beer; I was overwhelmed by the feeling to quit. All of my friends on the beach thought I was crazy. I thought, *What's new? That seems to be my life.* All of us decided to stay the night one time up the river near the waterfalls. This was when I started to notice that I wanted to sing a prayerlike song to the universe. I felt a huge difference in me, including the fact that I quit drinking alcohol.

I never did make it to see my friend in Belize. It was one of my dreams to do so one day, even if I was thirty-odd years late. He ended up getting married there and stayed with his newfound family. I just thought it would be so cool to end up at his door one day and say, "Well, here I am, a bit late, but I made it to meet you in Belize."

IDAHO

When I went back to Salt Spring Island, my bus was still waiting, facing the south with the windows open a bit. The warm sun prevented it from getting that mildew smell. I really started to notice what was wrong with other people. I started doing massages but never touched people and would only need to scan them with my hands. For instance, something would tell me what was wrong with them, such as their kidneys needed some work.

At this time, groups of people were going to the States to attend a healing gathering, and they asked me to come. I thought, *Well, why not?* So a few of us from Salt Spring Island went to a place called Brightonbush, Idaho. When we got there, they had a tent with all the workshops written on a blackboard. One of my friends and I went to take a look, and as we looked at the board, she said, "Isn't that what you do?" She was looking at a workshop that said something like spiritual healing. A man who was in charge came over and asked what we did.

I said, "I have no idea, it seems I have a spirit guide that tells me what is wrong with people."

He said, "Why not put your name down and see if anybody signs up for a treatment?" I put my name down but had funny thoughts about doing so.

A little later I went back and there were four names by my name, so I wrote on the board that was all I would accept. I met the first person in the area where people would do their work on people, an area sectioned off by curtains and small massage tables. I did three treatments and every one of them said that was exactly what their other healers said was wrong with them. It made me feel good about what I was doing, which I really didn't know. The time came for my fourth appointment and when she showed up, I asked her if it would be all right to do the treatment out in the middle of the field. There was a beautiful grassy field in the middle of everything, and the sun was shining brightly. So off we went for the treatment. She laid down right in the middle of the field, I knelt beside her and started running my heart-side hand over her body. When I got to her solar plexus area, I told her that there was something there, and I didn't think I could deal with it.

Boom, it hit me like a ton of bricks, knocking me over onto the grass. Something came into me via my solar plexus. Before I knew it, I couldn't sit up, let alone stand up. Black stuff started running down my leg coming from my rectum. I felt all the energy leaving me while at the same time she just got up and walked away. I started slithering toward the river; I thought if I could just get to the river, I would be able to get rid of this intruder. As I slithered, my "spirit guide" (what I called it for lack of better words) kept saying, "We can help you, we can help you, and all you need to do is give it back." I kept thinking, *I can get rid of this; all I need to do is get to the river.* As I dragged myself along, black stuff kept coming out of me, and I felt my whole life force leave me. I could hear the rushing waters of the river. I thought, *If I could only make it to the river.*

The voice kept telling me, "We can help. Let us help you." I finally made it to the river with enough strength that remained to grab a small tree and roll myself into the river. It was too late; I felt my life force leaving, and everything started going before my eyes from my lifetime here on earth. I thought of my children and how my job wasn't yet done. I said to no one in particular, "Help me, help me. It isn't mine to deal with."

My spirit guide started telling me what to do as I somehow ended up on the riverbank and crumpled up like a dirty old grain sack. The spirit started telling me to breathe, pray for good energy from above, and breathe through the crown chakra in a clockwise motion. During that time, it wanted me to hold for a count of eight, and then pray about what I was going to do with my breath. I was praying like crazy that I could give this energy back to this woman.

The spirit went on, "Now after you have held your breath and prayed about what you are going to do with it, let it out through your mouth and have the tip of your tongue on the roof of your mouth. When you let it out, visualize it going in a clockwise manner through your body." I visualized a corkscrew cleaning everything out as it went. I did this a few times, and the voice said, "Now visualize the woman, and when you breathe out, push the energy toward her." The energy had nowhere else to go but back to her; after all, it was her energy to deal with, not mine. So I started visualizing where she was and when I felt the time was right, I let the breath out, directing it to my solar plexus, and pushed the energy toward her. I was totally overwhelmed by the results. As soon as the breath left me, I got up and walked away as if nothing had happened. I never saw that woman again, and she was nowhere to be found on the grounds of the healing gathering. I learned a lot through this experience in many ways. Number one was to learn how to protect myself. I also knew after learning this breath that I could have dealt with whatever came into me through that woman.

Oh yeah, I have got to tell you this. At the gathering there was a guy who lived and worked with a guru from India. He was a real cool guy. He came into the sauna with a couple of other people, and three of us happened to be lucky enough to be in there at the time. He told us that he would like to share a chant with us. So we all sat cross-legged on the floor and chanted, "Om," and in no time we were all levitating off the floor, I kid you not. I had never experienced something like that again in all of my travels. If I remember right, the guru he trained under was BaBaGee, although I'm not entirely sure.

But we all sure had a great time. I ended up catching a bus back because my ride was going farther south in the States. The funny thing was that at the gathering we ate nothing but good food for days. I was shocked that when the bus stopped, many of the people from the gathering instantly went to McDonalds.

MY DREAM HOUSE

When I came home, it was finally time to buy a share in the Mill Farm. The benefactor had a couple of shares to sell because people defaulted on their payments and gave the one-tenth interest in the cooperative commune back to her.

Then, the fun began. However, deciding on a site was not an easy task since all the good sites had already been taken. Personally, a site with a view was number one in importance and water was second. Finally, I picked a site near the back meadow, which was an easy part. Right away some people commented on how close the site was to the meadow and the volleyball court. It seemed that some people just wanted to say no. I couldn't get started on my cabin before their own dreams. After countless meetings with a quorum and some without, I finally got the approval from the number of shareholders in order to get my site approved. After receiving approval from all ten group members, in 1983 I started developing my plan that had been a lifelong dream.

My plan was to build a home using just the surrounding environment as much as possible. During that time, my priority was to clear small trees for a garden and a building site. The first thing that I did was clear a spot for my school bus. Once the bus was there, I bought an old cast iron tub. I situated it between rocks high enough off the ground to have a fire underneath for a bath. The water was hot, but the bottom of the tub was unbearable, so I placed boards underneath the water and sat on them while bathing. Although this was a hassle, it kept the skin on my bottom intact after I finished. The experience was pure bliss for me to be on the mountain. I spent most of my time on the hill, which was a convenient term to use when referring to the Mill Farm. I had always felt a spiritual connection to the mountain in many ways. Even when we first came to the island, I would spend most of my time looking out over the hills, to be in the light. The location that I chose to build my home had the beginnings of a free-form rock foundation in the hillside. A friend of mine drove his tractor over the mountain to skid the logs close to the building site. I peeled most of the logs myself in order to use them as the framing material for my house.

Growing up in the foothills of Alberta, where I could only see the curvature of the earth from my homestead, I realized that I needed to live where I could see beyond the horizon. The site that I chose made this possible. This was during the time of my life when I started opening up to the other side, especially after the healing gathering in Idaho. I still remember when my grandmother came to me in a dream, riding in a blue van with a five-point gold star painted on the back of it. After my grandmother came to me in such a profound way, I started my quest where I met many incredible people during my travels in order to learn more about my dreams.

After my scary experience with the bus, I was afraid to go up a steep hill again. The bus was parked on the trail below the site. I really wanted to drive the bus up the steep grade behind the site. The day finally came when I built up enough courage to drive the bus up the steep grade. I put the old girl in first gear, which was real low, and proceeded to drive it upward. Without a hitch, the bus made it to the top of the building site. The view from my land was unbelievable; it looked over Samson Narrows, Cowichan Bay, and Satellite Channel. This peaceful bliss lifted my heart to the colorful sunsets in the west.

It seemed to take forever to get the foundation done. Once it was completed, the log framework went skyward in a hurry. In those days, there were a lot of trees that got blown down onto the road. I would get a friend of mine to load them up into his truck and take them to his place near Fulford. He had a sawmill and would cut the trees into boards for flooring and sheathing for my dream home.

The bottom floor that was close proximity to the earth was made out of sawdust. I used all the shavings from the logs and mixed it with cement instead of using gravel to make the ground floor. Believe it or not, it made a very good floor, which was a bit dusty at first. However after sealing it with paint, there were no more problems with the dust. During the rockwork, I had seen a lizard that was about ten inches long. I am glad that I took a picture of that lizard because I had never seen anything like it before.

SPIRIT MOVING OBJECTS

After seeing a spirit move objects in Yelapa, I came home one day to the bus. I opened the door and saw something in a bag that was on my couch. I couldn't believe my eyes—it was a bag containing my old scout badges. When I was fifteen, I left my mom a paper bag of all my favorite possessions, including my scout badges. This was the first time that I had seen them since the day I left them with my mom. What puzzled me the most was remembering that when I was around nineteen, I asked my mom for the bag, and she said she lost it during their move. Come to think about it, this was the only time in my life that I can remember getting mad at my mom. In the end, I found it amazing that all this was happening to me, and I had to find someone to talk to about spirits moving objects.

I was finally living my dream. I never really realized until now how my working trip to Vancouver changed my whole life after meeting a man on the ferry. The reason I am sharing a lot of these stories is because in 1996 I was told to start sharing them as much as possible.

I remember when I went to Vancouver to help my ex-father-in-law paint an apartment in the west end of the city. He always gave me a ride to the ferry. At that time, there was no sky train or fancy transportation, which made it hard to get to the ferry. I remember something that came to me in a dream and told me that I had to catch the bus to the ferry. So I quickly woke up my ex-father-in-law and told him that I had to leave even when we weren't quite done with the painting job. I understood, but I had to leave straight away in order to catch the bus. He was totally bewildered with my request because I usually would have completed the job and got a ride to the ferry. There wasn't much he could do, for I was determined to catch the bus to the ferry.

I walked up to the bus stop very early in the morning to catch the first bus. It went along a route and stopped at a hotel in Richmond. The bus was pretty full at that time and a man of First Nations descent got onto the bus. He looked amazing with his long black hair, which flowed to his waist in a thick braid.

In a hurry, I got on the ferry and went to the café. I stood in a huge line up. Being an old ferry traveler, I looked over to the other side where there was no one in line and proceeded to go over there. As I was walking along the corridor to where the trays were, I noticed only one other person ahead of me: the man with long braids that shined in the bright lights. We hit it off instantly, and it was the fastest ferry trip ever. I felt comfortable enough to tell him about Yelapa and some of the things that had been happening to me. He said that he would pray for me and asked where I lived. He later mentioned that he had a sister who lived on Salt Spring Island with her husband. I am having a bit of a hard time writing this as we speak, but I think the reader needs to know this to really understand the story.

At this point, I was a single dad for about two years. My ex-wife wasn't able to have the children because of her lifestyle. In the beginning, I went to a lawyer when she left, who mentioned that he could write up legal documents because she left the matrimonial home and the children. But I didn't want to make out any legal papers at that time.

After approximately two years, I received a phone call asking if the children could come see her at her dad's home in Vancouver. She sounded fine, so I agreed to allow her to have the children for a few days. After all, my children were wondering whatever happened to their mother. After a few days, I talked to the children, and they said they were coming home and to meet them at the ferry in Fulford Harbour. So here I'm standing and waiting for my children to get off the ferry. I didn't see them coming down the pathway with the other foot passengers. A stranger came up to me and asked if I was Bruce Williams. I said yes, and she handed me a big brown envelope, turned around, and walked back onto the ferry.

Yes, you guessed right, I was being served with court documents. They were custody orders, and I had to appear in court. I knew my ex-wife knew that I would never show up because I don't like courts. Not showing up meant that I gave my ex-wife custody of my children. In this legal agreement, it stated that our house would be sold and the proceeds split. In the end, that is what happened and how I bought my share of the Mill Farm Cooperative.

There, I got that off my mind. Now to get on with my story.

I stayed in the mountain like a hermit at this time, just praying and thinking about every thing imaginable. My main thoughts were circling around my encounters with the First Nations man and trying to find his sister on Salt Spring Island. I got myself back together and walked over to the mountain. I never had insurance on my truck and didn't want to drive it to the north end where the sister lived. The First Nations man also told me that he had a friend who lived near Blackburn Lake.

To my amazement, I was able to find the sister and her partner at home near Walkers Hook on the north end of Salt Spring. We all hit it off right away; they loved my stories and answered my question on spirits that could move objects. They told me many stories of spirits moving objects to get people's attention. One thing I learned was that spirits like a person who is a clean vessel to use; that's why I gave up drinking. During my visit, the sister had a migraine headache, so I prayed and told her that I would try to help her with it. I did my breathing that the spirit showed me and prayed for the earth to take away her headaches. I have used that breath for many things, especially on myself; even when I feel like something is coming on, I just pray and breathe. Like I said, I use the corkscrew as a visual; sand paper also works well. When working on someone, I would visualize along with the breath. So I did my breathing, and before I knew it, she felt better with no headache.

I had to go across the mountain to help my girlfriend with a fire; she had a permit and was burning during fire season. She lived near Cushion Lake, and when I arrived, we got the brush pile going. All of a sudden I had a feeling that the First Nations man was close by and trying to get my attention. I told my girlfriend that I had to go right now, and she could not believe what she was hearing. I knew that the man was trying to get in touch with me, and I had to go. So off I went in search of him. I walked up Blackburn Lake Road toward Cranberry Mountain. He never told me where except that it was near Blackburn Lake and up the mountain. Thank goodness there weren't many houses at the time. I knocked on a couple of doors, but no luck. Then I walked by a house I knew—it was an old radio broadcaster's house, so I knew it wasn't that one. I came to Cranberry Road and saw a driveway, so up I went. I knocked on the door and waited for what seemed like forever. Then the door opened and there he stood, my newfound friend. He told me that he had been calling me.

I said, "Yes, I know because I got your message." He wanted to get a hold of me because he was having a pipe ceremony and needed help building a sweat lodge. I had no problem with helping, not even thinking about my girlfriend with the fire going down on Cushion Lake. After all, this was a spirit getting in touch with me in ways that I had only heard about. In my mind this was what I had been praying about, so I was going to follow it and do what I had been praying for.

Building the sweat lodge was truly an amazing experience. He taught me everything as he prayed and offered smoked tobacco. He wanted me to be his fire keeper, which I was more than willing to do. We gathered the firewood, and the grandfather lava stones were already in place, which someone had brought from off the island. Just when it was getting dark, he started the sacred fire to heat the stones, after offering them many prayers. As the fire keeper, I took a fork and moved the burning sticks of wood aside, got a stone on the fork, and slid the stone through the door, where someone would take the antler horns and place the stone gently into the pit. He had so many stones to do four rounds. Once the stones were inside, he would say, "All my relations," and I would close the door. I stood outside watching the fire and made sure that all the stones were covered with wood per his instructions. When I heard the call, "All my relations," I would open the door to a blast of steam. The people inside would come out for a break between rounds and give me thanks for standing guard over them and watching the fire. This went on for three rounds, and after I put the stones in for the fourth round, he said that I could come in and close the door behind me.

My first round ever in a sweat lodge felt so good, and the cedar boughs that adorned the floor smelled so succulent. He gave me a little bag to hold to my third eye. It was truly an amazing experience; I had already quit drinking booze when my spirit guide came to me in Mexico. However, I had smoked pot every day since 1966, and this was around 1982. He said in the lodge that it would be easy to quit smoking pot; all I needed to do was pray. In 1966

I quit smoking three packs of Buckingham Plain cigarettes a day, but after being sick in bed for a week, I replaced the cigs with marijuana. I really wanted to follow this, what they call the "red road," so I prayed and asked for help to stop smoking pot, which I did at that very moment in time.

I stayed the night and had my first pipe ceremony, which was a very powerful experience. I got a ride with them to the south end, where he was catching a ferry back to where his other sister lived, outside of Victoria. I noticed some of my friends, and they were looking at me in a strange way. I asked one of them what was up with the weird look. They said go look in the mirror, which I did, and wow, I saw a huge red circle where my third eye was. It looked wide open. My prayers were answered, and I never had any problems with smoking marijuana. At that time, there was no phone service in the area and no computers. The only way for me to communicate was through the use of moccasin telegraph, which worked very well when my new friend, Milton, wanted to get a hold of me.

Spirits were coming into my life like crazy. For instance, when my girlfriend was staying over one night, a spirit came into the bus in a ball of white light. When the light dissipated, there was a spirit standing there in a black, hooded robe. The spirit had no face or feet, which I learned that it meant the spirit was from a different world. Another time, I was alone in my bus, and it filled up with the most amazing rose smell. Yet, for some reason, I was afraid. I had to go ask about these things. I thought to myself that Milton's sister would have the answer for sure. So the next time I saw her, I asked her about the rose smell. She told me that it meant that a spirit had just crossed over and was coming to me for help. Lesson after lesson, I was learning about this new journey that I was partaking in. I learned to pay more attention than ever. She taught me to say my name and ask them who they are and why did they come to me. The sister told me to talk to them as if they are right in front of me.

We started traveling up country together into the interior to participate in spiritual gatherings. For example, one time we went to the Stein River gathering in Lytton. Milton would ask me to go into the water early every morning and introduce myself to the water spirits. The man who organized the event in Lytton asked Milton if he and some of the other pipe carriers who showed up would do pipe ceremonies all along the road to where the Stein River met the Fraser. To get to the other side of the Fraser River, you had to take a ferry that operated totally on the current of the river. I was very happy indeed to help with anything I could. It became known that I could take away people's sicknesses. A man of First Nations descent, who was very famous at the time and had written a book, asked if I could help him. I said sure and took away the sickness that was ailing him. At this point, I had no idea where all this was going to lead me.

EDGEWOOD MEDICINE WHEEL

That summer, I went to a medicine wheel near Nakusp, BC, which was a small gathering where I had met a man who became a very good friend to me over the years. He was starting on the same path and had just lost his son to an accident that he felt responsible for. I tried sharing a lot of the things with him that I had learned. I cannot mention a lot of their names because, bless them, most of them have gone to a better place now.

One night, my girlfriend, who would come to stay and help me with the land, witnessed what I had seen. Just before we went to bed, I blew the candle out in the bus, and a few minutes later it came back on. That was the last time she stayed in my bus. She said that there were too many weird things happening there, and she couldn't handle it anymore. She would not stay in the bus again.

We all sat in a circle, which wasn't very big at the time, and contained maybe twenty-five people. I was sitting there cross-legged and prayed to the wondrous mystery, asking why I had never found a four-leaf clover. Then, all of a sudden, when I looked between my legs, there was a four-leaf, five-leaf, and even a six-leaf clover. When it became my turn and the feather was passed off to me, I showed the multiple-leaf clovers to the people participating in the circle. I still have them pressed in between the pages of a book.

I later told the circle about the time when we went to bed and blew out the candle, and it came back on ten minutes later. Across the circle, I saw an old man with gray hair smiling and laughing to himself. I said the words, "All my relations," and passed the feather on. When the feather reached the old man, he laughed out loud because it was his turn. He told everyone that he wondered who the young man was that Milton was talking about. He mentioned that he was at a pipe ceremony at Milton's home outside Victoria. Milton asked if there was any fire going in the house, and someone said that there was a fire going in the basement, in the propane furnace. Milton then asked everyone to concentrate on the fire. Milton told the group that he had met a young man a few months back who lived in a bus with no power, on the side of the mountain on the isolated side of Salt Spring Island. He then wanted the group to all think hard about the fire in the furnace and transfer that energy to light his candle. I thought to myself, *What kind of people have I met through my prayers for the understanding of my life?* This was truly an amazing realization that I thought was just a coincidence. I soon learned that there was no such thing as a coincidence.

In this circle, I met a man who carried eagle medicine who was from the South in the United States. He said that he was getting a message that he should carry the eagle medicine for this medicine wheel. He carried two golden eagle heads that had been in his family for years. He wanted me to carry one, so he presented this to me in the circle to carry the golden eagle's head for the Edgewood medicine wheel. What was happening to me? It was like a dream, and I wondered when was I going to wake up. Someone pinch me to see if it is reality. I met a lot of powerful people at that wheel. There was always laughter to be heard everywhere through the camp. When I came home, all I could do was go up the mountain and pray, which I did a lot. All along I was slowly building my cabin etched into the mountainside.

We were called to the Bonaparte Reserve to do a sweat for a brother who was a singer. There were two medicine men from Arizona who had some special medicine for cancer. The medicine was a root of the lily plant. All I could think of was, *Man, do they have huge roots.* The roots were mixed with fungus of the willow tree and made into a tea. We had four sweats there close to Marble Canyon. Oh, I just remembered my son was with me at the time. He went off hunting deer with one of the kids, up the mountainside, which was across the road.

I still kept the fire and was only allowed to go in on the fourth round. Back then that was how it was done; you would tend the fire for some time. I often watched and learned everything that went on, and I never even considered going in the lodge. The lodges all had a reason; someone would give tobacco, and we would build a lodge with those prayers. When the lodge was done, we would burn all the willows, prayer ties, and the cedar boughs on the floor, to send those prayers to the creator. When we threw the prayer ties in, we would then turn our backs because we weren't supposed to see what came out of them. I was certainly learning a lot about spirituality in a big way, directly from the heart.

My spirit was flying on cloud nine. I was invited to many different gatherings, sweat lodges, and circles, which were becoming a normal way of life for me. I was always taken care of financially for the work I did for the people. You were never to ask for any money ever. However, there was always a wad of bills rolled up and stuck in my front pocket.

Then the message came through Milton's sister. She asked if I want to go to Fairbanks, Alaska, to an indigenous pipe carriers gathering of North and South America. There would be five of us going in a Dodge van with the back altered so that we could stand up. So off we went from Victoria. We drove straight through for five days and nights. It wasn't long before this that a sister gave me a people's pipe to carry. Milton had just come home from Sun Dance and offered me a stem that he danced with, for my pipe. It was an amazing stem made out of cedar and looked very old and well used. I sure started learning about the power of the pipe ceremony. At that time, we were having pipe ceremonies a lot because people were always giving us tobacco and wanting prayers.

Anyway, off to Alaska we went. The hard thing was whenever we went into a new territory, we would stop and introduce ourselves to the water. We stopped along the way where we knew there were sweat lodges. There were some up near Williams Lake and Quesnel. Thinking about it, we did stop in a few places along the way, even a sweat at a huge lodge near Lake Labarge in the Yukon. After five days and nights on the road, we made it to Fairbanks, Alaska.

The first day we got there, an old man latched onto me and wouldn't go with his caregivers. The man was 104 years old. The gathering was amazing. The people wanted to figure out some long-standing issue that needed to be resolved. So they had a circle for days, twenty-four hours a day. When you left the circle, you would leave your energy there, and no one else would take your place. The woman who ran the circle wore a coat made out of eight generations of her grandmother's hair. She had a talking stick with white eagle feathers on it. This was a gift that Milton brought from Vancouver Island. After the first day of the circle, she would just hold the talking stick out, and it would go across the circle to the person who she wanted to talk to, and the eagle feathers would follow in the air. I remembered the old man was always by my side. I could understand everything he said, whereas no one else could. Later, for some reason, Milton's sister wanted to go home early, and there they caught a ride back home. Just after they left, the old woman with the jacket told us how to transport ourselves to a different place. All I could think about was Milton's sister and her partner; they left just when things were heating up. So I visualized myself going down the road and coming across them in a van to tell them about what I had just learned. It was about six months later when I would see them next. When I saw them, they both mentioned that they had seen me sitting cross-legged and coming in one window and going out the other.

There was drumming, hoop dancing, and a welcome round dance. The old guy defiantly wanted to go, so arm-in-arm we did one round of dancing. He was very proud of himself for doing that round. I never knew that he was one of the keynote speakers. How did this ever happen to me? They had called him up, and of course I got to take him onto the platform stage with a microphone. He started talking and no one could understand him, so I had to interpret for him. That was the last day of the gathering, and I cannot forget telling you about my meeting with our teacher and an old Cree lady from Saskatchewan.

She told Milton and me where she lived in Surrey, and that she wanted us to come by and stay with her for a while. She shared the teachings of the pipe with us. So we said "see you later" to everyone, and when we were about to leave, we realized that the old man was supposed go with the people who brought him. But he wanted us to take him home, so we did. That's when the real problems started, when we arrived at his reserve near Tok, Alaska. He urged me to stay with him, but I had no money, only my backpack and pipe. I guess I had already earned my first white eagle feather that the old woman gave me from the talking stick. I asked Milton what I should do; he never had to say a word. I knew by the look in his eyes. So here I'm on a reservation in Alaska, staying with a 104-year-old man. I soon realized one of the things he wanted most was to have a pipe ceremony at his home. I stayed with him for quite a while and listened with a clear mind and heart. I took in all his teachings. One of the main things he told me was to sit in the northern doorway at any ceremony, and then he would be able to find me after he left this world. Still to this day, I sit in the northern doorway of any lodge or ceremony I'm at.

The old man told me that before he went hunting, he would pray before going out into the wilderness. Every footstep that I take, prayers go to the one above every minute of the day. He shot his last moose at the age of ninety-six; now that has to be inspiration not to be a couch potato. When he was a young man, he would take a piece of Tamara, sharpen the end, and then put it in a fire, which would burn it to a point where it would be rock hard. This was what he would take with him to go into the bush for protection along with his bow and arrows. I never thought about bears until he told me an amazing story. One day the old man went out hunting and missed the trail of a black bear, ending up in between a mother and her cubs—yes, she had triplets. The bear immediately charged him, and at just the right moment, he took the spear and jammed the blunt end into the ground. He knelt down and held it at the right angle, so that when the bear lunged at him the spear went into the bear's throat, puncturing the jugular vein. The bear clawed at the spear and bled out immediately. To watch this wrinkled, withered old man tell his story was beyond words; his eyes sparkled like a young boy's.

Before I forget, I had a dream the night before that took place in False Creek, Vancouver. There was a little island in Burrard Inlet that the orca whales were washing up onto and having a very hard time surviving. In the dream there was a group of us that traveled north in my school bus, and on the side of the bus were the words, "Vision of Light." The whales were happy when we all got on the bus and went back into the ocean.

I got up one day to make us some breakfast, and as we sat there, the old man told me that I had been here long enough. I couldn't imagine in my wildest dreams what the old man was going to say next. The wrinkled old man sat there telling me in his language that it was time.

"Time?" I asked.

He said, "Yes, it is time, for you have been here long enough now." I knew in my heart that I had earned an amazing eagle feather from the old man. He gave me an eagle feather that he had had for many years. Even to this day, I still carry that feather close to me at all times. Then he said, "It is time that we get you a wife." Oh man, this was just too much. I was lost for words, and I told him about my dream about saving the whales. I knew I had to follow my dreams and go home to get the bus ready. I needed to come back to get the old man and begin to travel south with the Vision of Light. He was very sad to see me go as I got into the car with some friends that came from Tok, Alaska, to give me a ride to town.

At that time, I had no money, so I stayed with my friends in Tok where I would go out to the road and hitchhike. I had done this a lot over the years. However, this had to be the worst, and it wasn't the lack of traffic out there. I stood on the side of the road for three solid days. It was like a job; I stood there with my thumb out and a big smile on my face. When it started to get dark, I walked over to my friend's house and ate supper, visited, and went to bed. The next day, my friends would make me a lunch and off I went to the roadside. On the fourth day, I thought back to my earlier years hitching, remembering about how I would go to Husky service stations and ask drivers for a lift. I never even went to my spot on the road and instead walked over to the service station. I really prayed hard that morning, and my prayers were answered. The first car I asked agreed to take me only to Beaver Lodge where they were headed, but at least it got me across the border. The lights went on, even at that time in the early eighties; people didn't want to pick you up just before the border. I had no idea that the border was only about twenty miles away. Once I got across the border and got dropped off on the roadside, I got a ride right away with a guy in a truck that was going to Vancouver. He wanted to drive straight through and picked me up to drive while he slept.

VISION OF LIGHT

When I got back onto the island, all I could think of was my dream about the whales and going back up to Alaska to get the old man. So I began to remodel the bus in order to carry nine people, which meant it was going to be mainly sleeping spaces. I started telling people right away about my dream and wondered who would be interested in such a trip. To my surprise, Milton and some of his friends thought it was a great idea and wanted to come along. The plan was just to pray every day and stop where the spirit wanted us to. I had my son at that time, and when he turned twelve years old, he came to live with me. It was his choice legally, no matter what the courts and my ex-wife thought. So I got him enrolled in a correspondence course.

Milton was a member of the Baha'i faith. The members liked my plan and wanted to support our endeavor, but only if I became a Baha'i. At first, I had a hard time with this decision; however, since I had never gone to church, I decided to join their organization. Little did I know the turmoil this was going to create for my son and myself.

People came to Salt Spring Island to get on the Vision of Light bus. The send-off was great, with all the local Baha'i being there. Every day we would start the day with prayers and a smudge to clear the way. If someone had a vision, we would follow it to the community where we felt prayers and help were needed. We would always find the chief or an old person who was one of the main figures in the local community. Most places we went to were on reservations. We would give them tobacco and ask them permission to come into their community. A lot of time they would thank us and say it was just what they had been praying for. We would start out by having a circle, which later led into a sweat lodge ceremony.

The reader has to understand that during this time a lot of reserves never had a sweat lodge ceremony and never wanted one. Some would only allow a circle to happen or a pipe ceremony, but not a sweat lodge because they thought it was a prairie ceremony and didn't belong in their territory. Things sure have changed since those times; now you can see sweat lodges right beside the long houses on many reserves. We always prayed for guidance and help with providing us with food and gas. No matter where we went or when we left, there was always a wad of cash in our pockets along with dried fish, meat, and preserves for our trip when we left their community.

Things were going along real well. We hit Sugar Cane Reserve just outside Williams Lake and had a great sweat lodge experience there with a friend that I had met at the medicine wheel near Nakusp, British Columbia. I was unaware of what was going on, but this is where things started going wrong. My girlfriend wanted to meet up with us, so I thought why not and gave her directions of where to meet up with us.

Our next leg of our journey was a long one, and it was getting cold; after all, it was November. We were invited to come to Bella Coola, but we only had enough money for gas and our food stash was running low. It was so cold that I had to keep the stove on in the bus as we traveled. People would give us strange looks when they drove by for the stove pipe came out one of the bus windows with smoke billowing out of it.

We would sing and drum as we rolled along, and some people did their crafts as well. Prayers were always in our hearts and spoken out loud. We always asked to be taken care of, especially now that we had no food. As we went across the plateau toward Bella Coola, it started to snow heavily, and the road was slippery. We were about to go down this huge hill toward Bella Coola when we saw a truck in the ditch as we went around a sharp curve. Not to worry, someone else had already reported it. You could see that other trucks had stopped and picked up boxes of food. It was a truck that was delivering food that rolled off the road, spreading food everywhere in the snow. We started picking up dried almonds, apricots, and all kinds of stuff in the snow and putting it in the bus. Our shelves were full of food as we pulled away from the overturned truck.

The energy of Bella Coola was very odd and different from other places we had visited. Their teachings were different from most we had ran across. They showed us a top of a mountain that was squared off. They said it was to guide their ancestors when the world was flooded. The old people said that they came from across the big waters in a boat. That squared-off mountaintop guided their people there many years before. We had some very good circles there. However, it was the first time that I noticed people's strangeness toward my son, Orin. The members said that was no way for a young man to live, traveling in a bus and not going to school, and that I should leave my son there with them while I was on this journey.

Our next stop was Quesnel. Some of the people on the bus knew a family there that was willing to accommodate us. I would always stay in the bus because I loved my space. At some of these stops, we would be involved with the local Baha'i community. Quesnel was great. There was a sweat lodge outside of Quesnel that we would fire up, and it seemed like every day we were having a sweat. People couldn't get enough of it.

We went to the local Baha'i place one day, and they called me into the office. They told me that they could no longer support the Vision of Light and myself because I was traveling with a woman and we were unmarried. I couldn't believe what I was hearing. I just never thought of things like that. I realized that was what all the talk about my son in Bella Coola was. They thought it was not proper at all to be traveling with a thirteen-year-old and not be married.

Oh, I remember it well. I had little money, and we decided to move to Alberta where I used to have the farm at Hoadley. We figured we could get work in Alberta. We stayed in the bus by a friend's farm, and then we found an old farm with a trailer on it to rent. My son went to the local school where he went when he was in grade one. I remember having no money because it was Christmas time, and I wanted to get my son a set of drums. I think they were $150 back then, and that is all we had. My girlfriend and I had a little conversation about this one. I really wanted my son to have something, so we bought the drums. It is funny that while I write this, I realized back in 1982 I had no money. When we split the house proceeds, I bought the Mill Farm and the school bus. My girlfriend went to work in a camp right away as a cook, so I was a single dad again. Which was fun because my old farm friends would always invite us to dinner.

All I could think about was getting back to Salt Spring Island and the Mill Farm. I also thought about the old man up in Alaska a lot also. I managed to get some work driving a truck and was able to save a few bucks. As soon as the snow was gone and school had ended, we went back to British Columbia. My Alberta friends were surprised when I left to go back to the coast. They had never seen or known about the mountain and how much I had taken it into my heart.

I kind of felt jilted or whatever you call it. My heart ached big-time over being rejected after all the hard work I had done in many ways for my newfound friends, the Baha'i. My whole life was always torn apart because I never felt I belonged anywhere. When I got back to Salt Spring Island, I never got back in touch with any of my Baha'i friends, which included Milton. I never felt that I belonged to any groups anyway, so I just really got into the mountain. To top all this off, I was the crazy guy who lived on the mountain, coupled with the fact that I never drank alcohol or smoked pot anymore.

PROSPECTOR

I was becoming very fond of rocks and the geology of the mountain. A friend told me that if I took the prospectors course, he would hire me afterward, which meant that he would take me to the Yukon to work in the spring. My girlfriend just kept doing her own thing, and I guess all I could say was, "It is what it is."

When I went over to Victoria to take the prospectors course, Kimi, my wife, was working over there. One day I saw her and asked if she wanted to go play tennis in order to stimulate the pineal gland. She said sure. That is really the only time we saw each other before I went up north. Oh yeah, by the way, all we did was stimulate our pineal glands in the sunshine, while playing a good game of tennis.

Then I graduated from the prospector's course and off to Yukon I went. I called it my "all found job," and I never took my wallet out for six months. My boss rented a van, which we loaded up with boxes of supplies that I made in his shop. The boxes were designed to be lifted up in nets by helicopters for fly-in camps. We drove for three days north until we hit Ross River, Yukon, which was on the Robert Campbell Highway. We set up camp on Bruce Lake outside Ross River. We brought some geology students up with us to work as dirt baggers for the summer. We started doing lines right away, just off the Robert Campbell Highway. The whole area was covered in a layer of volcanic ash from thirteen hundred years ago.

Do you think we could tell these guys not to sample the ash? The object was to go below the ash and get an actual soil sample. I really think it just came down to laziness; they were unwilling to dig deeper and would always just bring ash back. It was a tough job if you weren't used to it. The city's geology students didn't last more than a week. One guy even came back to camp going on about being chased by a bear and that he was traumatized and had to go back to Vancouver. We knew he was telling a fib because he told us that he went up a tree to get away from a black bear. The best thing about the students leaving is that we were able to hire local guys, three young men from Ross River. They were fantastic to work with and knew what we wanted them to do. I was called the crew chief, which also meant I was the main prospector. When the boys were out soil sampling on their reports, they would say there was an outcrop of rock at such and such point. So it was my job to go out behind them and to take rock chip samples, log them, and put the samples into a bag. These were collected along with the soil samples and flown to the lab in North Vancouver to be tested for any mineral content that the samples might contain.

The day finally came to start our fly-in camps. This was what we were all hoping for. The geologist and I would always fly in on a recognized flight to find a good place to set our base camp. Number one was water. We would set up a gravity water feed system in order for us to have running water for our kitchen and shower. We bought one of those demand hot water propane heaters. It sure was nice to come back to camp and have a hot shower and meal. The daughter of the geologist came along with us to be a camp cook.

Our camp consisted of wall tents. For example, the kitchen had a metal frame and was fourteen feet by twenty-four feet in dimension. Yes, we flew in everything by helicopter, even our stoves, fridges, tables, showers, and anything else we needed. Then we'd set up the kitchen and shower. It was up to the men to set their own tents up. There were two men to a nine-by-twelve wall tent. The geologist never would get us stoves for our tents, so we had to make our own out of old metal oil containers that we would find in abandoned camps. It was very cold in the mountains. Our camps were above tree line, which was around six thousand feet above sea level. The good thing about this was the fact that there weren't any bugs at all. We would still get snow in June, July, and August up in those barren mountains that hosted glaciers and their incredible green-colored lakes of emerald shins of beauty.

We always had major differences with the geologist when we moved camp. I had my chainsaw and would always tell the pilot to drop me off near the tree line to get some firewood. It was very expensive wood; we figured about six hundred dollars a cord. The geologist finally started agreeing to this method of getting wood when one of the guys made him a stove for his tent. We also put one in the kitchen after weeks of sitting in there freezing when we went in to eat. Do I dare mention that he was a Scotsman and was always trying to scrimp on everything?

It was suppose to be a dry camp, until another prospector came into the camp from Ontario. He showed up with a bag full of booze while I sat there for a couple of hours watching everyone have fun. Then out came the bottle of whiskey, which was my weakness. I knew by drinking it that I would have to put my pipe aside; the old pang of drinking hit my emotional side, and I picked up the bottle, taking a long swig straight from it. The guys all looked at me in amazement, as they drank theirs mixed with Coke that the prospector brought in. That is the way I learned how to drink back in my Bowness days, straight from the bottle, ever since I was nine years old. The party went until the early hours. Even the geologist got into it. The next day was a very slow day indeed; there was only one guy who didn't make it out on the lines. The funny thing was, when we were out on the lines, we found the geologist passed out on a hillside, so we just let him sleep, jotting it down in our heads that we got one on him.

From that day on, whenever the helicopter came from town, there was always some booze somehow that got into the camp. People going out to the health center or to have a weekend visit with their families would sneak booze back into camp. It also became very obvious to all of us that the geologist was sitting in his tent at nighttime drinking scotch whiskey, something I could never drink. I tried it twice, and it hung down in the back of my throat and would exceedingly hang down on my tongue, making it very hard to swallow, so I never drank that stuff.

One night as the geologist went into his tent with his private scotch stash, one of the guys went over to his tent in a slow fashion and placed a tin plate on the geologist's chimney. It didn't take long until he got smoked out of his tent. He came out at a dead run. Going to the back of his tent, he saw the plate and started swearing like crazy, then started laughing. Finally, the ice was broken somehow and he became one of the boys. He was raised old school; they were taught that it was never good to become friends with the hired help.

We really had a lot of fun in those mountains. We walked up to caribou and saw grizzly bears and bighorn sheep. These were just a few of the daily sights. You had to be on your toes for bears, though. We carried bear spray all the time and also bear bangers, which didn't work well. The best thing to do with bears is carry a little metal flask with a marble in it. That is what I always did to make noise so that they knew you were coming. Better still, if

I ever saw signs of a bear, especially a grizzly, I would immediately turn around and leave the area, and I mean immediately. The best bear encounter I ever had—and I have had a few over the years, was when I was visiting my friend who lives on François Lake near Burns Lake. In fall, I was taking my morning walk and some black bears were around, eating berries. I was walking down the driveway toward a sharp ninety-degree corner. I turned into it at the same time a black bear did. We came face-to-face, and my automatic reaction was to lift up my arms and scream, but the big black bear turned right away and ran in the other direction. No, I didn't need toilet paper, but I was very close to needing it because I almost crapped my pants with a full load.

Some of the guys got to go to Ross River for the weekend, while some of us from other parts never got to go anywhere. After three months, I asked the geologist to give us a break from the isolation; after all, we had been working every day for three months solid for him.

The next time the helicopter came in, he threw me the keys to the van that sat in Ross River and said, "If anyone wants to take the weekend off, here are the keys to the van." Three of us never said a word and ran to our tents to pack our bags. In all my life, I never saw three people so excited. On the way to town, the chopper pilot took us through the Hoole River Canyon. Was that ever exciting! The jagged rock walls of the canyon seemed to be only inches away from us, and the rough rapids below looked close enough to wash the pontoons clean as we swept the surface of the rushing waters of the Hoole.

On the way to town, we decided to go to Dawson City; we'd heard it was the Las Vegas of the North. The pilot said it was about a six-hour drive away. My problem now was drinking, and so the first thing we did was buy beers on the way. The next thing we did was go to Diamond Tooth Gerties. They still had Can Can girls dancing there. It was a great show right out of the past. We even stopped to see some of the local sites, like Jack London's little log cabin. The amazing thing about Dawson City was the fact that it was one of the only old gold mining towns that never burned down, so all the old buildings were the originals, fixed up, of course. We went to see one of those old gold dredgers. Man, are they huge! Like three stories high. You could just feel the energy of the past bouncing out of the hallways and grabbing you like a ghost from the past, enveloping you into their world of yesterday. Gold fever was the tune, which the spirits danced to as their gold chains clanged in the hallways.

We decided to just hang out in the local bars and listen to the music. Things became a blur, and I crashed in the back of the van. When everyone finally showed up, it was back to Ross River we went, where the chopper would be waiting for us to fly us back to camp.

We would fly out from the main camp and spend a few nights in a smaller camp with just tents. We would do panning in creek beds for gold; the prospector from Ontario was with us. We followed a stream where we'd been getting showings in the pan. We would go up a creek and map it out. We came upon a rock outcrop just above where the showings were glittering in the bottom of our pans. This was no fool's gold; it was the real deal gold. The Ontario prospector took a sample of the bedrock and went crazy.

"We found the mother lode!" he started shouting at the top of his lungs. "All these years I have been prospecting and never have I seen a sample like this," he said. We had a radio so that we could talk to the main camp. He started going on and on to the geologist that it was the mother lode. I knew what he was going to say: was it found in Rhyolite? The client wanted to find gold in Rhyolite. That was his main purpose of this exploration. This guy didn't want to listen to the geologist and told us that he was a friend of the director of our main company. The guy wanted to get out of there to take it to Vancouver and show the director of an exploration company in Vancouver. He was like a raving lunatic, gone wild over finding the pot of gold at the end of the rainbow. He said that he was going up and getting another sample, and away he went up the creek. He was gone no time at all, and then we saw him running down, holding his hand, which was bundled up in his coat. He was screaming about how much it hurt. Man, this guy was crazy. He'd smashed his hand with the rock hammer. It was a bloody pulp. He said it was an accident, which we knew it wasn't. He said that he had to walk out to main camp. It was a twenty-four-hour walk; the days were long so there was a lot of light to see your way. So off he went. All we heard about when the chopper came for us in a few days, was the chopper flown out that nut case. Then when he got to Whitehorse, he flew directly to Vancouver with the gold sample in his bag to show the director. We never saw or heard about the guy again. The funny thing about this story was that we just learned that the other day that a company did came up in that area at a later date and did a lot of sampling through drilling some core samples as well.

A couple of times we got to go to Ross River when we moved our fly camp. Ross was like a boomtown at this time, and the hotels were always full. We were lucky to get one room. Can you imagine four men, bags full of stinking laundry, staying in one room? Consequently the bar sounded like more fun than hanging in a room with men sorting through dirty laundry. The bar was like out of nowhere, and fights were very common. I was more interested in the local stories. One main story goes, a man sat at the bar having a beer when his prospecting ex-partner walked in. As the man stood up from the bar to see what was the meaning of this intrusion, his partner who just walked in pulled a .45 caliber handgun out of the back of his waistband and quickly pulled the trigger, blowing a huge swath of blood and brain matter all over the bar. The shooter then sat down, asked for a beer, and said that the bartender had better phone the police, as he sat there calmly awaiting the local RCMP. The story goes that the dead man never put his partner's name on the documents, stating the fact that the undersigned person was the only prospector involved in finding a huge showing of zinc, which became a huge mine in the early '60s near Ross River and supplied most of the world with lead for car batteries.

The next story always makes me shake my head. It had just happened while we were out in the mountains. There was a local man who would break into the bar and help himself to beer and snacks. He pushed his unquenchable thirst late one night and broke into the bar on yet another occasion. The owner caught him red-handed, subdued him, and tied him up. He called a few friends instead of phoning the local police. His friends dragged themselves from their comfortable beds. There was a meeting in the dark and dingy bar with splintered wooden floors that creaked with every footstep. Their tools were a bottle of turpentine and a wire brush. After going over the entire scenario, one man pulled the man's pants down. Once his pants were down, they told him to bend over. As two men held him in that position one man took the wire brush and rubbed the thief's backside with the wire brush until it was streaming blood. The men then took the bottle of turpentine and poured the whole thing over the splintered floor. With his hands still tied to his front and screaming at the top of his lungs, they proceeded to drag the man across the floor like a floor mop. I don't even want to go there to think how that would make me feel. One thing for certain was the man never broke into that bar again.

The main thing that I would always buy when I went into town was Speed-Sew fabric glue because your pants would get worn out so fast, especially when you had lines going through buck brush. The brush would wear holes into your jeans very quickly. My jeans ended up just being one huge patch, and I knew how heavy they had become with all the patches by feeling the weight of it. It was getting close to the long weekend in September, which was our kick-off time to head back home.

PARTY TIME

We wanted to get home for the long weekend, which we did, and boy, did I ever have fun. The party was held in the old Harbour House on Salt Spring Island—some liked to call it the "Animal House." My newfound job was great. I had a huge check to come home to, and when I went to my bank, my savings totaled around $14,000, if I remember right. I had my sights on finishing my cabin up at the Mill Farm.

When we went through Vancouver, we stopped at an office on Howe Street to visit the main company my boss worked for. While we were sitting there, I started reading this report that was in front of me on a glass coffee table. It had a reflection of the fish in the nearby water tank that seemed to be suspended on the wall. The tank also had a mirror on the back of it, which made it so that the reflections were always on the move and created an endless depth to it all.

I asked where this property was in the report, and the guy said, "It's where you guys were working."

I said, "That's funny; I never was part of any core sampling." The two men towering over me just exchanged glances. You have to remember this is back in the day of the Vancouver Stock Exchange, where anything and everything went on. I told my friend as we drove to the ferry on our way home after months of being away that I would never work for that company again, now that I'd read the falsified reports.

I was silent on the subject when it came to being a pipe carrier, in the teachings we had received. When the two of us went to the old Cree woman's house in Surrey, she shared many teachings of the pipe with us for two whole days. One of the main teachings was that you have to put your pipe away if you drink alcohol or do drugs. So at the time I put my pipe away, which meant I didn't even touch it or show it at all. Basically, I was back in my old habits; in other words, the party was on.

You have to remember that times were different, and as a young lad in Alberta there was a group of us that would always get jobs together. We had an agreement as soon as we could fill the trunk of my friend's old 1959 Pontiac half-full of beer and half-full of whiskey, we would quit our jobs and the party would be on. For the life of me, I still have a hard time remembering some of those weeks gone by without the memory of those binges. It's funny now looking back and editing this part, that I met one of these guys on my last trip to Victoria after fifty-one years. It seemed just like yesterday.

So it was in my blood. Once the party was on, look out, I went to town, which just meant going down the hill to the Fulford Inn. At that time, I drove an old international pick-up truck, which I hadn't insured for eight years. Many times I would be driving home and when I got too tired, I just turned the truck off and went to sleep. In those days there was hardly any traffic on Musgrave Road.

Before I knew it I had three girlfriends who liked to party with the best of them. It was getting close to Halloween boogie time in Beaver Point Hall. For twenty-odd years it didn't matter where you were, you made it to the Beaver Point Hall Halloween boogie. A lot of local musicians, some of whom were famous, would get together and play their hearts out for us. It was at this dance that I had a date with a woman dressed as the bride from hell, though I ended up dancing a slow dance with a man in a suit who ended up being my wife.

She told me that the Mill Farm was always her dream, too, and those words were the key to my heart. The fact that one of the first times that we walked up to my cabin on the mountain, we saw two eagles mating. They were so enraptured with what they were doing that they fell to the earth, landing in the trees right beside my cabin. We both thought this had to be a message to us. I proposed that evening to my wife-to-be. No, I didn't get down on my knees, but she said yes regardless.

It was very nice for me to have someone to plan my dreams with, which turned into our dreams. The first thing that my new wife suggested was to tear the new roof off, and build the cabin higher by adding another floor to both increase the view and have the kitchen and living area on the second floor instead of the ground floor. On the top would be another room, which would be our bedroom. It was very hard for me to tear off that new roof, but the new plans did make a lot of sense, so we decided to tear it off. That was in the fall of 1988.

We wanted to get our new dream home built so that we could move in right away. Since I'm a glass man, we used a lot of glass and had a lot of window space. First, we framed the whole place with logs. I would take the chainsaw and cut a grove in the upright logs, creating a slot to slip the glass into. This was a nice effect, making the view exceptional with no interference from window framing, which could block the breathtaking view across Samson's Narrows.

We were so excited to be living out our dream that we moved into the first floor once the new floor and roof were added. When it snowed that winter, we awoke with snow on our bed. That was how unfinished our new home was when we moved in. Someone stole our cast iron bathtub while I was away working, so we came up with a new plan for a bath. We would heat up water in a big pot on the wood stove, bring the wheelbarrow into the house, and fill it with water. This was how my future wife bathed before she drove over the hill to work as a nurse. After she was finished we would just roll the wheelbarrow outside and dump out the water.

Since I was going to be a married man again, we talked about what I was going to do for work. I didn't want to go away from the island to work anymore, so we decided to start Fulford Glass. I talked to Bruce Patterson and asked him if I could use his old shed beside his house to have a glass business. He said sure, if I was willing to clean it out. It was a lot of fun for him seeing all of his grandfather's old stuff from the past. Before I go into the Mill Farm story any further, I had better tell you part of the story of how I ended up on Salt Spring Island in the first place.

SLOCAN VALLEY

I always wanted to go and live off the land; it was a personal dream of mine. That coupled with the fact that I was into the '60s hippie way of life made living sustainably seem very fitting in many ways.

I was a member of the glaziers union in 1969, which then went on strike. They informed us that they were calling in a shop vote: if you voted to continue work at the shop you worked for, you could keep working. The union agent, a fat, ruddy-faced little man, came walking into our shop one day, where I worked in Terrace, BC. He said, "You guys need to pay twenty-five percent of your gross wages into the strike fund."

I looked into his baggy eyes, at how the folds of his sleepless gray ran into blotched stained cheeks of ruddiness, and replied, "You've got to be kidding, why do you think we voted to work in the first place?"

He shook his fat little stub of a finger at me and told us we have to pay; it's all about being a brother in this union and taking care of the ones on the picket lines. As his butt, which was broader than an ax, disappeared out the door, I said to myself, *Good luck, bud.* A few months later, after the strike was over, he turned up at our shop again and said we are going to take that 25 percent off your paycheck. I asked my boss if he could do that and he said it was out of his control; the powerful union could take it right off your check.

I said, "Well, that's it for me, I'm heading to the Slocan to buy a little piece of land for myself." He wasn't happy at all but understood how I felt. We left Terrace in the late '60s and headed to the Slocan Valley. We were actually some of the few Canadians at that time in the Slocan Valley. Most of our friends were draft dodgers from the States and the local Doukhobors who had been in the valley for many years.

The American draft dodgers' parents would send them money to live on. Many of them would pool their resources together and live in a communal environment. One group, called the Red, White, and Blue Circus, would come by and try to get us to join their commune. The women were young and beautiful. The first thing that happened is they would peel all their clothes off, which was a common occurrence in the valley in those days. Then the sales pitch would come: If you join our commune, you can be anything you want. If you wear a white button, you swing both ways; a red one meant you liked females, and a blue one meant you were liked males. The potluck parties in the Slocan were a bit of a gamble in those times. *Do I eat a dessert or not?* That was always my question. Sometimes you would eat a dessert and have a two-day trip that would be a mind-bending experience, to say the least. No wonder the local band in those days was called Brain Dead.

Our swimming hole was downstream from the Appledale Bridge on the Slocan River, and on a sunny day there would be fifty bare-naked hippies rolling around in the mud and having the time of their lives. Local Doukhobors would complain about it, but it was funny how the Doukhobor men would be on the bridge looking at the naked sights with binoculars.

How I found out about the Slocan Valley was that I had placed the glass in the Selkirk College in the mid-1960s. On weekends we would go on tours of the area, and I fell in love with the Slocan. On one of those trips we went down to the States to a place called Kellogg, Idaho. I was about eighteen at the time. We looked for a place to stay that night and found ourselves in an old hotel that was all there was at that time. We were told to sit on this bench and about six half-naked, boob-toting babes strutted their wares by us, smiling at us like we were the best-looking guys in the universe. We had no idea what Kellogg was all about; it seemed like it was trapped in the late 1800s. After going through the same routine in four other places, including one that asked me for ID, we had our eyes full of exploding boobs trying to pop out of their skimpy lace tops with dangling frills and G-strings. We headed back toward the Canadian Border where we knew the lay of the land.

The Slocan was a very cooperative type of community in those days. The energy of the old Doukhobors who lived communally for many years permeated onto the very ground we lived on. Everyone would cooperate with one another. Someone would have a chainsaw, another person had a truck; it was amazing how fast we would get our wood in for the winter when everyone worked together. We bought five acres that included a stream running through it with top water rights, a garden, and various sheds. Some of the sheds were the ones that Japanese prisoners of war were interned in at Lemon Creek.

One of the first things I did was buy an old Jersey milk cow from a neighbor, along with chickens. I wanted to get right into living off the land. There is nothing like getting up early in the morning, especially when it is cold out, and snuggling up to a warm cow to get fresh milk. That milk can be turned into many by products, such as butter, yogurt, sour cream, and cottage cheese. One of the best ways to make butter, we learned from the old Doukhobors, was to take a glass gallon jar, put that rich Jersey cream in, and just roll it over your knee. In less than an hour you would have thick, creamy butter.

When I met old Early, an African American man who lived in Trail, I thought I was the luckiest man alive to have met someone like him. I met him on a cool spring day with snow still on the ground. His twenty acres were covered with trucks, Caterpillars, and every type of machinery known to man. Inside his old house, which only had a pathway through it, were old Wurlitzer jukeboxes, welders, toolboxes—you name it, it was there. At the end of the cluttered aisle of paraphernalia sat an old black man hunched over a wood cook stove. His gray beard was burned back to the skin line of his pocked, scarred face of eighty-four years. When he nodded out, his steel-wool beard would rest on the top of the stove, searing it to a color of burned brown.

He awoke from a deep sleep, his raspy voice uttering, "Who the hell goes there?" The hair stood up at the back of my neck, making me trip over a cable winch lying on the floor. George introduced me to old Early. I still marvel at the size of the hand that came out to shake mine. It felt like alligator skin and was as big as a baseball mitt.

He said, "Damn, I hate those doctors, stayed away from them all my life. Got a little cold the other night and my foot slipped out of my bedding, buddy took me to the hospital, and the bastards cut my toe off, gave me some kind of cock-and-bull story that if they didn't do that, I would get gonorrhea. I told those stupid buggers we are talking about my toe, not my dick." Then he laughed from deep down, a bassist guttural sound that I had never heard before. It made me love the old black guy right away.

Early bought five acres of raw land right beside a piece of land I had, built an A frame on it and sold it to Paul. Early asked us if we would help him move, once the snow was gone, and George and I said sure and that we would ask our friends to help. It was a huge job moving all his stuff to the five acres of raw land, on the edge of the forest facing south above the Slocan River. He had a flat area cleared before we started the move. Everything went under tarps. The first thing he asked us to do was to dig a deep hole for a temporary power pole. It was a hard dig because the hillside was still part of a once great glacier left over from the ice age glaciers of ten thousand years ago.

We showed up the next morning and saw the hole was all filled in. When we asked why, old Early said that it was in the wrong place and he wanted it on the other side. Right away I thought to myself, the old bugger buried his stash in that hole. During the move Early would pay us with old King George twenty-dollar bills. He never trusted anyone, including doctors, lawyers, governments, or the banks.

He bought a few lifts of cedar from the Slocan sawmill. At that time, a "lift" would be fifty dollars and would consist of approximately two thousand board feet of cedar. This cedar is what all of us would build everything out of in the valley. In our old house, I built a god's eye on the main wall out of that cedar, it was beautiful. We set up Early's old cook stove outside, beside his tent.

When we asked him if he would be OK, he said, "Hell, I spent three winters in the northern states in a tent dug four feet into the ground that was covered in snow. Don't you young bucks go worry about the likes of me, you hear?"

I would take Early milk, eggs, butter, chicken, and pork, everything that we produced, plus garden produce. I realize as I write this that old man supported us in a major way at that time. He would put everything on top of the stove, including fresh chicken; he would never eat it until it was a few days old and sour. No wonder he never got sick: there were no bacteria in the world that could take that grizzled old man on.

During this time, a few of us would get together to build him his shack, which was about sixteen feet by sixteen feet. Once we finished it, framed it, put a door and roof on, and built a chimney, Early moved in—with no insulation and nothing done on the inside. It immediately resembled his old house in Trail, so full to the brim that it had little trails to the stove and the bed. He put his welder, come-alongs, and tubes in the house because he swore they were the most important things for his perpetual motion machine. That was Early's favorite thing to talk about, his perpetual motion invention. He had lead balls, tubes, and all kinds of old scrap metals for his invention. It gives me great strength as I write this to never give up on your dream. That old man sure never gave up on his dream.

I was very happy Marcus lived next to Early because he could check on him. Marcus was another "back to the lander" from Toronto. He was so green that I had to show him how to change the oil in his Volvo. He told me he was going to go back to Toronto to become a lawyer, then to be a politician. He thought that was the only way that he could ever make a difference, through the political system. A few years later I got a gold-embossed letterhead from Marcus, who had become the minister of education. He said he made it but still couldn't make any difference to the system because he had to follow the party line.

Early one morning in the winter, Marcus came walking into our house with a ghastly look on his unfurrowed youthful face.

"I think the old man is dead," he said. When I went over that morning, he was lying there cold and still like that old Caterpillar of his that never moved. Marcus said it looked like he fell and hit his head. We went to a neighbor and called Doctor Bob—the dropout doctor from San Francisco who set up a practice in the valley.

We went up to Early's and looked around. Nothing looked out of place at all. You never thought of those kinds of things back then, like foul play. Needless to say, everything was in place.

When Doctor Bob arrived, he said, "Yep, he's dead all right. You had better call the funeral home in Nelson. They'll come and take the body away. I'll write up a death certificate.

Later that day when the undertakers arrived, there were a couple of our other friends there; word traveled fast in the valley. The men brought a big black rubbery body bag with them and were about to stuff Early in it.

I called out, "Hold it! We will do that." I knew the old guy would've wanted it that way. What an experience that was to put a lifeless, six-foot-plus, big-boned, grizzled toting corpse into a bag. That was the easy part; now we had to carry him down Early's famous path to the black hearse below.

Early had his own ways, and the way he made a path in the snow was the Early way. He would have two five-gallon buckets with ropes on them and put his big feet in them. The funny thing was that his toes would be scrunched up in the bottom of the pail, and when he took them off after walking and tramping the snow down to create a packed-down path, it was the funniest thing to see him cursing the Early curse trying to get his feet out of those buckets. Many tears roll down my face as I write this, thinking of how lucky I was to meet the character of Early Whitley. Anyway, carrying him down that path was no easy task; we would slip off the side and into snow up to our waists. And trying to get back onto the path was no easy task. We finally got smart and just pulled him like a sled down the path with the two black suits, whelping like a bunch of young pups in our wake in the snow.

The next day we went to Nelson to arrange everything for Early, and we were surprised when the RCMP told us they couldn't find any record of Early's family and asked us if we could help with that. We said sure. We went to Trail and asked the post office for any info they had. They told us that he never got any mail whatsoever, which never surprised us in the least. After a few days of inquiries from our side and the authorities, we all came up with absolutely no family info for our old black friend.

What happened next was very disconcerting to us all in many ways, especially when we thought of Early's hate for the government in general. They said because there was no family on record, the sheriff was going to put a certificate on his door, seize everything, sell the property, and that all the proceeds would go to the government. The minute we heard that we took off out of there like a lightning bolt was about to strike us down. Marcus and I started planning right away what was going to happen before they put the lock on his door. Besides us, there were three other guys who helped Early a lot with both the move and building his cabin. Deep down in our hearts, we knew this was the way our old friend would want it. On our way through the valley, we told the other three friends what happened and to meet right away at Early's.

Once we were all there, we talked and decided that anybody who wanted anything of Early's better take it now and be gone with it. The thing I took was the ax he used to cut his wood with, that was it, and I still have that ax some forty years later. There was one big problem because one of the local guys found out what had happened, and he was very pissed because he had his eye on the welder, which one of Early's buddies took. The old man had owed him some money for work he had done.

Marcus and I went to the funeral home in Nelson and were very surprised to learn that they were going to put Early in a plywood casket, which they referred to as a pauper's funeral. The hair stood up on the back of my neck when I heard those words.

I said, "There is no way that he is going to be buried as a pauper, Mister Undertaker. The Crown is selling his land and possessions for a tidy some of dollars. We want him to be buried in the best casket you have and be clothed in a tuxedo and have a stone grave marker. That old black guy you are burying is no pauper. We will do anything we can to see that this is done right."

To our surprise he said he understood totally and would get the paperwork signed by the government agent and give Early a top-class funeral. It was a small service with just his close buddies as pallbearers, and we were just so happy to see the old man in a fancy tuxedo and a fancy casket, with a smile seemingly on his face, laid to rest.

HOADLEY

It wasn't long after this that we decided that we were going to move to Hoadley, Alberta, to have a bigger piece of land. The five acres in Winlaw just didn't seem big enough to live on. But the main reason was that I started noticing how I would go a bit crazy in the winter, because where we lived in the valley was very closed-in, and I would be walking to the top of the mountains on nice days trying to see out. It wasn't until later that I figured out why a lot of our American friends would go to California for the winter. Where I was born in Alberta, you could see the curvature of the earth and see the sunrise and sunset. In the valley you never saw a sunrise or sunset. I was always told it was a good idea to be able to see the sun rise and set from your camp site.

So we sold our five acres in Winlaw to Corky Evans, who later became a member of the BC Legislature, and loaded all our stuff onto a three-ton truck I had bought and headed out to Hoadley, Alberta. It was quite the picture, this old 1962 three-ton Chevy truck loaded to the gunnels with all types of stuff hanging out, with our basset hound and coyote-malamute mixed dog standing on top of the load. When we got to Hoadley, we traded the truck and $4,000 for 160 acres of land with old buildings on it. There was no power in the area at the time. We had to haul water from a spring in the summer; the winter was so cold that a glass of water froze by our bedside. It was a real learning curve in lifestyle coming from the pot-smoking Slocan Valley to the backwoods of whiskey-drinking Alberta.

One of our closest neighbors was a trapper and his family of nine children. The first time we visited them in their shiplap floor with cracks open to the darkness below, the old trapper sat down in his chair with his gun over his knee, chewing on a wad of tobacco that dripped down his chin of gray, stubbly whiskers. I saw his eyes dart to the side at the same moment the gun went off with an ear-piercing ring, echoing like it would never stop. A big smile spread across his face as he swiped at his dripping brown chew of tobacco with the biggest hand I have ever seen.

He said, “That is the fourth of the day,” as he scooped up a mouse, adding to no one in particular, “You won’t be coming back here any time too soon, you little bugger.”

When we visited them, it was always something that we had never experienced before. Like the time their boy came home from the rigs. We could see the dust from his truck settle on everything possible. He walked right up to his old dad, not saying a word, and hit his dad closed-fist as hard as he could, right on the old trapper’s jaw.

He just looked at his boy, said, “Hmm,” and knocked him out with one punch, so that the limp body flew across the room. The old trapper said, “Better luck next time, son.” As the son staggered to his feet, they shook hands as if nothing had ever happened. Then we all sat down to eat—you never knew what you were going to eat there—and that day it was bear ribs.

We always had a little knot in our stomachs as we sat down to eating in their home. Visions of the old guy digging out the fresh contents of his outhouse—yes, you heard me right, not aged over the years—then shoveling it into a stone boat, toilet paper and all, still stick in my head. With a team of horses pulling the stone boat, he would shovel the contents from the outhouse onto their garden patch, I kid you not. The old trapper still walks the streets of Rimbey. He has to be in his late eighties now.

It sure made it hard to eat any potatoes and carrots that came with your meal in that house. There was also another problem when eating, if pork was served. As a trapper, he would bring his animals home that he had trapped and skin them in the house. Then one of the kids would drag the carcass outside and throw it into the pigpen. The pigs would go crazy over the carcasses.

He had a real problem with the young lads who lived next door, which was about one and a half miles away. They were always so excited to come home from work that they sped by his house in a cloud of dust, which would drift right into their front room. So what does the old guy do? He gets his .30-30 rifle and shoots a tire out from the speeding truck. Well, this really added fuel to a war that had started a long time ago. No one was on the old trapper's side with this stunt, which could have ended in a serious accident. So what does he do next? He digs a trench across the gravel road to make us all slow down when going by his place. The local road department and the cops came, telling him enough is enough. They could never fix that trench there, though, and there was always a little bump as you went by their farmstead.

We lived next to an old family that homesteaded in the area back in the day when you could get land for free as long as you worked it and turned it into a farm. There was a great deal of history in Canada that still had to be told in many of our so-called backwoods areas. Some of the early homesteaders came from the States and were on the run from the law. Many of the families there had always kept their pasts locked away in an impermeable, invisible secret family vault. You combine this along with the fact that some people had Indian blood in their background, which also has been a secret in many Canadian families, and it makes for a lot of stories that have yet to be written about the true history of this mysterious land we call Canada.

One of the stories that was most interesting to me, which I had heard about both in my travels and by hearing families talk about it, was the Great Depression. Many farmers in those days made moonshine; it was the only way they made it through those rough economic times. Underneath the few eggs and cream they would take to town to sell would be hidden some pure grain alcohol, which was traded to the local merchants for the main staples the farmers needed. It was kept a secret because pretty much everyone in the local community was involved one way or another with the distribution of illegal booze. Our neighbors to the north had five sons who were always trying to get me to drink their whiskey. I never drank at this time, but I did smoke my ditch of weed, which I grew myself. Neighbors and even the RCMP who came by to see a tractor I had for sale never once batted an eye when they walked by my greenhouse, full of the holy herb.

The boys thought it would be great if we had a present for moving into the neighborhood, after we had fixed up an old homestead house on the land. When I got up in the morning, I found there was a pail of honey that weighed thirty pounds and a bag of squawking chickens. I thought, *Great, where did they come from?* I knew it had to be the Marten boys who for sure stole them from someone's hen house. My mind swirled around in a sea of paranoia, people would think, "We got a chicken thief in the neighborhood, it must be that new guy with a ponytail!" I could hear them saying that. So I grabbed the bag of chickens and dragged them to the road because we had no driveway at the time. I took them to a farm a few miles away and let them out. When I returned it was light out and there were chicken feathers all over the place so I spent most of the morning trying to pick up every sign that a chicken had been at my place.

The Marten boys were always over at our place; they were very interested in people who weren't rednecks. It was Christmas time and they were trying again to get me to drink their whiskey, so I said, "Yes, if you guys will smoke my pot." Well, they lit up like shining stars and said sure. The pot went right to their heads, and the oldest one passed out on my step. As he lay there passed out in his bare feet, I realized I needed somewhere to relieve my bladder—after all, they had given me a lot of whiskey—so I did so on his feet. His younger brothers were hollering how he would kill me, but I never heard a word and whizzed on.

Back to our house: we really needed a driveway, which would have cost a fair bit to hire a local cat to do the job. The county had to build a new multiplate culvert on one of their roads close to where my farm was. I told the political councilor of our area that I knew how to do that, so we made a deal to do a trade. I would build their culvert, and then they would build me a driveway. What an incredible deal that was. To make that type of trade would be impossible anywhere else except here, living out on the fringe of this gray-wooded land, on the edge of the Crown land.

To make money, I worked out of the house whenever I could, but I always wanted to stay home. Thus, we got into raising animals for a living, which went well seasonally but never provided a steady income. Then I got the bright idea to milk cows like some of the neighbors did (at that time, people shipped cream in cans to the dairy). It was a great living, milking four cows by hand, separating the milk and putting the cream out at the gate to be picked up once a week. Life was great; I had steady checks coming in and no bills.

Then the government started giving us a quota for fluid milk and wanted to get rid of the cream cans and have us make milk parlors and milk the cows with machines. That meant investing in a lot of equipment and buying even more cows to pay the bank. When I milked by hand, I would get paid for the quality of the cream, and I always got top dollars because my bacteria count would be in the range of eight thousand. We went from milking four cows by hand to milking twenty-two cows with the old pail Surge milking machines, which ran on a vacuum pump system. My first shipment of milk through the bulk tank and all those plastic lines came back with a bacteria count of 290,000. This was high enough for me to get the second level of the pricing level.

You have to understand that they shipped all the milk in the same truck, so just before they picked it up, they took a sample in a little jar before they mixed it with all the rest of the milk. There are way too many chemicals in the dairy business, in both cleaning solutions and via the drugs injected into the cows. They even have a warning saying that any product from the injected animal should not be consumed or drank for six months. So what most farmers do is put a gallon of bleach in their tank before the driver comes and mixes it all together. The timing is perfect and the driver gets a good sample, which is very beneficial to the farmer, especially financially! Then they took the milk and boiled every bit of goodness out of it and added corn syrup and a whole bunch of other chemicals.

The dairy business changed a lot from what used to be just milking by hand and having a mellow life on the old farm. It transformed into a very hectic lifestyle, filled with stress in many different ways. I sure learned a lot about cattle though. I learned how to feed them special proteins through the food they ate, and also how to artificially inseminate the cows. My friend who was a vet came over with a cow's uterus; he laid it out on a sawhorse and showed me how to inseminate a cow. So I bought a nitrogen tank and some fancy semen and bred my own cows.

I loved my life as a farmer. There were times I never went to town for over a year. However, even though I really enjoyed my life as a farmer, my wife at the time had different ideas. One of our friends had just come back from a place called Salt Spring Island.

Man, as I write this I can't help but think how I was so stupid at the time. I really was a sucker in many ways. I did what I did, and we decided to lease the farm and try out Salt Spring Island. This is after my wife at the time went to check it out with our friend from the Rimbey area. She came back saying she had seen a really nice place with log houses and all this cool stuff. All our friends from the Hoadley area were wondering, what is Bruce going to do? What could I do? We had two small children and I didn't want to separate, so we bought the house on Salt Spring. You have to remember that this was around 1977, so prices were pretty reasonable at the time.

We leased the farm out to a couple, which ended up filling my barn with concrete, making it into a pig barn. I had a whole collection of original LPs, like the first Jimi Hendrix, Led Zeppelin, the Doors, Cream, and so on. I had all of them. Plus I had many other things I collected like the first *Georgia Straight* magazines and cans of silver coins. The couple later left and took everything that wasn't nailed down.

SALT SPRING

The log house on Salt Spring Island was nice, but it never got the sun. I could not live without having the sunshine, so we sold it. I wanted to go back to the farm, so back we went. However, it didn't last very long, only a few months, and my wife at the time wanted to go back to the island. Consequently, we sold the farm lock, stock, and barrel, so to speak.

That was when we bought ten acres of land above Stoll Lake on the south end of Salt Spring Island for $17,000. I spent five months building our dream home, with a view of Fulford Harbour. I kept very busy, building houses and starting a glass business. Go figure, the name of the glass company was Glassy-eyed Productions I kid you not. It was South Salt Spring Island after all.

⸻

The house that I built on the hill was the one where I went home for lunch and my wife at the time left. Like I said, I should have realized something was up, but I didn't. Sometimes when you have your head in the clouds you think the people around you also have their heads in the same place.

Things were just getting started on the Mill Farm. There were four Mill farmers who got it together to have a living space for their homesteads. A single mother moved a big old school bus onto her site, and it wasn't long before she had another child. She was an amazing woman, how she persevered over the hill with those three children, which was a feat beyond most people's imagination.

Some people had no money, but a lot of determination. On one site the owner took all the small trees and branches, made a dome-type framework out of them, put a tarp over it, and piled more limbs and branches on them, creating a protected living space. You had to know it was there or else you would walk right by it. It was over the brow of a hill, fitting in perfectly with the contour of the land.

There were five sites that had all types of old building materials, piled up here and there under torn tarps that were blowing in the wind. Most people made good use of their trip over the hill and trucked in lumber, windows, stones, and basically anything to do with building. It all made its way over the mountain to be slowly put together, creating abodes with character beyond most people's imaginations. I was real busy trying to get our new house built and starting the new glass company, Fulford Glass and Aluminum Products. Many days I would think about my past life in many different ways and hear my grandma's words.

In my time, I had a lot of different jobs since I left home at fifteen to explore the world. My beloved grandmother always told me, "If you aren't going to go to school, my boy, travel's the best education you can get." The prospecting job was the best job of all that I had unless I include the ten-minute job I once had. When I was sixteen I got a construction job at Canada Packers. When I got there, they walked me through the existing meat plant. I had to walk on blood, and there were dead animals everywhere. When

I reached the outside of the building to the new construction site, I threw my lunch onto the roof and said I quit; I didn't want anything to do with that building. About a week later, I got a check in the mail for a day's work, which made it my shortest job ever.

THE WEDDING

In the meantime, while I was still building my dream cabin home at Mill Farm, reality was setting in, and the wedding date was set for July 16, 1989. We worked very hard trying to get the house together for this occasion. One of the biggest concerns was how to get my new wife's brother and sister to the house because they were paraplegics in wheelchairs. The house had to be as natural as possible, so when we built it, I didn't use a tape measure or a level at all. To level the floor, which was a ceiling in the first plan, I had just used my eye. Consequently, it ended up having a two-inch slope that ran straight toward a huge piece of glass and a ten-foot drop. The front of our home was floor-to-ceiling glass. We would joke that if Kimi's brother-in-law came into the house, he would roll down the slope of the floor and smash through the window.

Our wedding was the most beautiful occasion ever. We got our local musician friends to play live music at Beaver Point Hall. We also talked to Auntie Kate and asked if she could learn B. B. King's song "When Love Comes to Town" to sing at our wedding. Our home over the hill was a beehive of activity at the time as we tried to get everything ready for the wedding.

All of our six children helped get the place together. I remember that we stained the tongue-and-groove spruce floor the night before, hoping it would be dry for the wedding ceremony the next day. We arranged to have a justice of the peace come over the hill along with our family and a few friends. The place looked absolutely beautiful with flowers everywhere and the family all dressed up for the big occasion. My wife still ribs me once in a while about that day when I was saying my vows. Instead of saying "my lawfully wedded wife" I accidentally said "my *awfully* wedded wife." Which gets a chuckle still to this day when we talk about our union over the hill. Once our rings were in place we all carpooled down the hill to Beaver Point Hall.

Our friends did an incredible job decorating the hall, which was filled with tables covered by white tablecloths. On every table were a big vase of flowers and a huge loaf of braided bread, made by Kimi's friend Barb. This set the stage for the potluck supreme and the entry of my wife and me in our bare feet. We just had to get married in bare feet. It was a party that we all remember fondly, as the food and music was exceptional. Near the end Kimi sang me a song that still brings tears to my eyes when I think about it. We were the last ones to leave the hall. Everyone was waiting for us to go. We were having so much fun and we figured it's our party, so we are going to party to the end.

THE GLASS COMPANY

This was a very busy time of life for us. We were starting a new company and trying to make our home livable. Vehicles were a major problem; I couldn't possibly remember all of the trucks, cars, and motorcycles we have gone through over the years of traversing that hill. Getting snowed in happened quite frequently and was one of our favorite times.

Getting my wife to work was always an adventure. Sometimes we would have to walk two miles to the neighbors that lived on the ocean and catch a ride on their skiff to Burgone Bay. Then my wife would have to walk to the bottom of Lee's hill and hitchhike to the hospital. There were many times she would walk all the way over the hill in the snow. This usually took her about three hours after already working a twelve-hour shift in emergency.

My son had a friend from West Vancouver who came over once when we were snowed in. We left him for the day, and when we came home, he had started a fire in the stove. The problem was that the stove he started the fire in was just sitting in the middle of the room, not hooked up to the stovepipe. Thank goodness we arrived home in time to bring it to his attention that the stove wasn't hooked up. I always wondered what he was on. There was, after all, a stove upstairs all hooked up and ready to go.

One good story I remember was when we had a cousin visiting from Ottawa. We got snowed in when he was here. The snowstorm had brought down a lot of trees over the road. He had to catch the ferry to be in time to catch his flight. We always carried saws, axes, and whatever else we needed to get the job done to make the trip over the hill. So here we go in an old orange Volvo trying to get him to the ferry on time. Many times we had to stop and cut through trees to get another few feet. Once we made it over the hump past the Buddhist retreat, it was a downhill run. Everyone was hollering that there was only fifteen minutes left until ferry time.

I said, "OK, hang on, here we go."

Going under the snow-burdened saplings created a whiteout condition as the old car did the limbo dance under the trees. I don't know how that bucket of bolts stuck to the road. Then everyone screamed as a blown-down tree about eight inches thick suddenly blocked the road. My split-moment decision was to put my pedal to the metal, and we cascaded over the tree in a blurry flurry of snow. Fishtailing back and forth down the switch-back to the bare gravel road, with steam coming out of the engine compartment, we sped to the ferry. As we came down the hill to Fulford, the engine was screaming a painful song and as we pulled up to the ferry ramp, the car rumbled, snorted a stream of steam, and died. Our cousin immediately opened the door and puked on the ground, composed himself, and ran onto the ferry just as the ramp was being lifted. The workers lowered the ramp, and he made the ferry. I had just created another mountain car wreck for Marcott's salvage yard.

We all worked hard trying to get our mountain home together. I got a propane hot water heater, which meant we could retire the wheelbarrow bathtub, and my wife was elated to have running hot water. We put a plastic hose to a dug-out water basin above us to have gravity-flowing water. This made living without power possible, especially when we got a Powerhouse Paul's Pelton wheel. It was a big alternator for a truck that had plastic casing around a plastic disk wheel attached to the shaft. There is a small hole approximately three-sixteenths of an inch wide, which the one-inch pressurized water line forces itself through, creating a stream that is three-sixteenths of an inch wide with a lot of pressure to spin the wheel, spinning it fast enough to charge the battery. Hurrah, we had 12 volt lights and enough energy for a radio. This wasn't enough for movies, though; the only way for us to see a movie was to rent a video machine and a television. The storage battery never had enough power to run it all. What we would do was drive the car as close as we could to the house, then I would lift the hood and attach a cable to the battery that in turn would run our video machine and TV. There was one huge problem, though: the car had to be running at the time. Yes, you heard me right, we were sitting in the house watching a movie with the car running outside. It was always a joke when someone would come and visit us at this time because we could not hear them approach with all the noise going on around us.

We had just finished digging a hole under our home about three feet by three feet square and another three feet deep. I framed it off with pieces of wood and made concrete walls with a concrete bottom. I built a light metal box the size of a small fridge and attached a rope and pulley. An instant dumbwaiter was created to be our fridge. It actually worked very well keeping the butter, milk, and veggies cool. It definitely never got cold enough to use it as a freezer, though. I was brought up this way and always wanted to relive my childhood way of life. The dumb waiter fridge was high on the list. My business started going like gangbusters. Especially when my son graduated in the fall of '89 and came to work for me.

The glass business starting growing very fast; it went from my son and me to a fourteen-person shop. No, it wasn't in Bruce Patterson's garage in Fulford anymore. When it expanded that fast, we moved it to a large shop on Musgrave Road. One of the reasons things got so busy was that I started manufacturing windows that were thermally broken. At the time, a large supplier of aluminum windows went broke in Victoria. What I did makes me still shake my head. I got one of their windows, cut it up into all the parts I needed to make the window, got some ink and a blotter pad, and dipped each square end of the metal into the ink and stamped it on the blotter pad. It came out to five patterns, which I took over to Vancouver. I made an appointment with the aluminum extrusion company. I think what happened was that they already had the dies that the bankrupt company needed.

I was very surprised when they said, "Sure, we can do that no problem," and I was in business.

It was an amazing time, hiring Salt Spring Islanders and teaching them how to make windows for a growing housing market. I knew all the contractors on Salt Spring, and I knew they had no choice in a sense because they were the only good windows at the time that passed the building code. I even had to take the finished product to a company over in Vancouver that put them through tests. For the glass company, I leased a new Chevy S10 extended cab, which was great for the mountain road. Kimi, my wife, was building raised beds for flowers and vegetables and asked to borrow it one day to haul dirt from over the hill. Things went real well until the last load.

The last little hill to our home was very steep, and the only vehicle that could make it was a four-by-four. When you got to the top of the rise there was enough room to turn around, which Kimi did to unload the dirt. She unloaded it no problem, and when it was all cleaned out, she closed the tailgate and instantly down the hill went the truck, smashing into rocks and trees. I couldn't figure out where Kimi was after work. She was supposed to pick me up. It wasn't too long after that she showed up at the shop with the truck story. Kimi is a classy gal and had never driven an automatic. When she turned the motor off and put it in park, it must not have engaged totally into park. When she slammed the tailgate shut it must have been enough to send it cascading down the mountain. I phoned Ron to tow it over the hill. When we saw it, we thought for sure it was totaled right off the bat because it was smashed up real good, but ICBC said they would fix it.

These truck stories remind me of my grandmother, and what she would say when one of my aunts would get on the phone. When we first got a phone, it was a party line with sixteen people on it, and when one phone would ring, all the other lines would hear the ring tone. Every farm had a different ring chime; I think ours was two longs and a short. As a kid you wondered, what was the sense of having the different ring tones, because anytime there was a ring, all the local ladies would get on the line and listen in. A lot of the time they would just join in on the conversation. When my old aunt Sadie would get on the line, bless her soul, my grandmother would say forget about trying to use the phone because when Aunt Sadie is on the line she goes on and on; it's like wiping your arse with a wagon wheel: you have no hope of getting on the line.

This saying is exactly how this story would go if I started telling the reader about all of our truck and car stories. And believe me, it was hard enough wiping my you-know-what in those days with old Sears catalogs in the outhouse. Talking about outhouses, our first mountain outhouse sat on the brow of the hill in a very precarious position.

THE OUTHOUSE

After Kimi's mom's passing, her dad brought an old family friend from Vesuvius over the hill for a visit to see where we lived. Kimi kept saying, "I hope she doesn't need to use the outhouse." But sure enough, right away she asked where she could go to the bathroom. Kimi said, "I will give you a hand," so off they went to the outhouse.

Later Kimi said we have to build a new outhouse and proceeded to tell the story of taking her dad's friend on a trip to ours. I never put a door on any outhouse I have built, and over the years I have built quite a few of them in my quest of getting back to the land. The reason I don't put a door on is that they are always situated where the beautiful vista is. The Mill Farm vista was the best of all. The problem was Kimi's dad's friend couldn't get up the hill to the outhouse, and Kimi had to push her up the hill to the outhouse. When she got to the point where she could grab onto something to pull herself into the outhouse, she grabbed onto the seat, which wasn't attached to the floor. Each time Kimi pushed her, trying to help get her into the outhouse, the frame that held the toilet seat would come right off the floor, and her head would actually go into the hole of the outhouse.

After that episode, I started building a new composting outhouse. I started by pouring a cement slab base for the foundation so that it would be easy to clean. It had two seats like we always wanted to have. There was a skylight in it along with a window, and of course there wasn't a door. The deal was that after you did your business in the potty, you would throw some peat moss and agriculture lime on your excrement. Every week I would clean it out and place everyone's business into a forty-five-gallon steel barrel behind the outhouse. It only took one year for it to break down so that it looked like soil and had no odor whatsoever. For some reason our girls loved the outhouse and would hang out in there. I think the real reason was to smoke, but we always kidded that we should have built one with four holes.

The pond in the back meadow was the most popular spot for our children to hang out. It was a game for them that every day, no matter what the weather conditions were, they would go for a swim in the pond, which was cold because it was spring fed from the bottom. It had to be a very nice day before it was warm enough to hang out in it for any amount of time.

For a few months we were getting lumber together to build a deck in the front of our home. Once we had all the material together, it was worker-bee time. It is amazing the amount of work you can get done with a few people, and of course a lot of beer and good food. At the front of the deck it was twelve feet off the ground. We framed it in with four-by-six uprights and two-by-eight joists on sixteen-inch centers. Once it was framed in, which only took a day, it sat for a year with no deck covering, just the framework exposed to the weather. Everyone said you have to cover that deck; otherwise it will go rotten. The expense of covering it would cost a lot, and I wasn't sure what to use for material.

Since I was in the glass business, I had all kinds of glass available to me. I just happened to have enough three-eighths-inch tempered glass to cover the whole deck. Yes, believe it or not, that is what we did: we covered the whole deck in tempered glass. People were scared at first to walk on it, but once they did and saw that it wouldn't break, everyone loved being on the deck. Looking over Separation Point and watching the sunsets became a nightly occurrence.

One night my son's dog came running onto the deck when it was wet. When he put his brakes on, he just kept sliding right over the edge to the ground thirteen feet below. She landed on the flowerbed, got up and ran off as if nothing had happened. I never did put a railing up because I didn't want to spoil the view.

My son got a bunch of his friends together, and in one week they built a cabin above our house. It was nice to have Orin so close by. I guess they took it seriously once their nest was built into the mountainside, because my son's partner soon became pregnant. Kimi and I went to Mexico a month before the baby's due date. Everyone was so worried we would miss the birth. I kid you not, the night we got home, our son's partner went into labor. We rushed to Lady Minto Hospital, where my wife worked. She put her nurse's gear on to help, and I became the hot-water carrier. What a blessing to take part in your first grandchild's birth! The mother and new baby girl were just fine after a short labor.

It's hard to sit here and write this in some ways, but I need to get this story out. I quit drinking that day because I never wanted my grandchild to see me drunk. Just before my granddaughter was born, we went to the opening of a job we just finished in Ganges. My son and his friend came with us and sat in the back in those jumper seats. The next morning when I went to work I noticed a scratch and dent on the truck. Right away I blamed my son and his friend for damaging the truck and not telling me. They said they didn't do it, and my wife went along with them. A week went by; I was still ranting about how could they have done this and not tell me. Finally they told me, they were giving me time to try and remember that when we came home that night, we went off the road. I put it in four-wheel drive and drove it out, damaged and all. So after this story, I thought, *It is time I really stop drinking.* Over the years I have had my ups and downs with drinking. Before this time, I fell off the wagon when I went to Ross River in the Yukon with the locals. So by having this vision of not having my granddaughter see me drunk has been great for me and has continued on to include my great grandson.

Our little homestead over the hill started to be the real thing. Gardens were flourishing, babies crying, and people's happiness ringing out like a song of joy rustling through the forest. Our sons and in-laws announced they were coming for a visit from Halifax. We invited them for supper; Kimi was working days, so I got the orders to cook the roast. I wrapped it in tin foil along with onions and garlic inside. Lighting was never a bright occurrence in our home, and candles were always our number-one choice for light. When Kimi came home, she wanted to see what the roast looked like, picked it up, and accidentally dropped it to the floor. We quickly scooped it up and put it back in the oven, thinking all along about the ten-second rule.

We were excited to use our new table, which we framed with logs and made a clear cedar bottom on it with the cedar from the beach that we split by hand. On top of the cedar we put seashells, rocks, and various treasurers. Then we put a piece of three-foot-by-eight-foot, three-eighths-inch tempered glass on the top to make the tabletop. Indeed, it made quite a big table for our large family.

Everything went well when the in-laws arrived, considering I have never seen my son so nervous. When we sat down to eat, my wife said we had better get some napkins, so I went to the drawer that contained the cloth napkins. The drawer was a mouse haven with mouse droppings everywhere. I nonchalantly shook them out with no one seeing what I was doing and proceeded hopefully to give each person a mouse-dropping-free napkin. Thank goodness for candlelight! We still have a good laugh over that episode. To this day I can't help but wonder that they had to have smelled the mouse odor on their napkins.

UNCLE TED

Mice and wasps were an unbelievable nuisance over the hill. The wasps got to be so bad that we left the top of the house for them. They seemed to understand that was their part of the house and left us alone downstairs. The mice, on the other hand, were everywhere. Not a nice feeling to have a mouse run over your face while you're sleeping. We tried everything possible to deal with the mouse problem. I think I'm plagued with a mouse problem; as I write, they are coming into my hut in Yukon.

The best trap I used was a five-gallon bucket with a wire through the center of a pop can. The wire was stretched across the center of the pail and tied on each side. Then you would put peanut butter on the can. You had to make a walkway out of a small piece of wood to within an inch of the peanut-buttered pop can, so when the mouse went to nibble on it, it fell into the bucket. A lot of people put water in the bottom of the pail and that would be the end of the mouse. Kimi would not have anything to do with the murder of a mouse, however, so we made ours a dry trap, and there wasn't any water at the bottom.

You could see that there were a lot of mouse activity, including droppings in the pail and tracks on the peanut butter, but no mice. So one day I sat there watching. I did this because it made me think of my old great uncle Ted, who lived all by himself in the foothills of Alberta in a small shack without a floor. At one end of the shack was a bathtub sitting on stones. All I ever saw him eat was peanuts. He would put all the shells under the tub and when there were enough peanut shells, it was bath time for old Uncle Ted.

Yes, his place smelled very strongly of smoke; the eave of the shack had a flap on it, which he would open for the smoke to drift out. Near the middle of the shack was a small table with old stovepipes around the table legs. Uncle Ted said he had mouse problems and couldn't figure out how the mice could get up on his table. So one night he watched and told us that the mice would crawl up the wall across the ceiling and drop onto his table. Never underestimate the smarts of a mouse. Funny, as I go over this story, I'm sitting in my own hut with a dirt floor.

So I sat there watching, thinking of my uncle Ted. Sure enough along came the mouse walking the plank, it took a little jump onto the peanut-butter-laden can and instantly fell into the five-gallon pail, which was approximately twenty inches high. I always thought it had to be impossible for them to get out, but the mouse started running around the bottom of the pail, and it was like he was using centrifugal force; he flew around the edge of that pail like he had a rocket booster attached to him and flew out of that pail, landed on the ground, and scampered off.

After that I put a skim of water at the bottom of the pail, which was just enough moisture to slow them down and not drown the little creatures. I would take the pail with me up the mountain and drop them in the bush, alive and healthy. Our children loved the mountain very much, and they always talk about how some of their best memories of their childhood were when they were able to spend time up the mountain.

Over the years, we often wondered when some of the other community members would come up to live on the Mill Farm. When would the group begin to build the community we had all dreamed of? So far only my family and our neighbor with the three children were using the land. While we were building our life over the hill, the Mill Farm meetings became less and less of an occurrence for most shareholders. A lot of people were losing interest when they found out that borrowing against the land was very hard to do under the current agreement.

COOPERATIVE SHARES SELL

What had happened to our dream? Cooperative laundry, school, workshop, orchards, and gardens had been planned. Three years had passed since we'd moved up the mountain—was it all just a quaint, naive notion? Every time shares changed hands, or a shareholder started a new relationship, new ideas emerged like a flow of lava over the mountain. With it came innumerable new ideas, issues, attitudes, values and beliefs, incorporation, subdivision, commercial logging, bylaws, constitutions, and tenants associations. The list goes on endlessly with all the ideas. Remember, some of these ideas were from members, not even owners.

In 1986, some of the first original partners left the Mill Farm Cooperative. These members' needs and priorities had changed over the years, and they wanted to get a mortgage against the property. They were refused when the bank realized that the community mandate would never achieve a unanimous approval to develop a subdivision. Unable to achieve their anticipated economic gains, they sold their shares in the Mill Farm Cooperative.

After the second original purchaser sold his share in 1989, it was clear that the remaining founders would need to present the new owners with a formal legal document that laid out the guidelines that were agreed upon by the original tenants in common. During that time, our benefactor who founded our community decided to sell her own three shares in the Mill Farm. Despite her best efforts, she was no longer able to lend her support. She gave us notice that she was going to sell her shares, and if any members were interested, they could purchase them.

A lot of us tried to put our heads together to either buy her shares or find like-minded people who would be interested in buying in. At the meetings, the discussion on buying her shares for the better interest of the Mill Farm always produced the same outcome: the majority said no. A meeting took place and the members decided that something had to be put in place while the original owners were still shareholders. We needed to get a legal set of bylaws to govern our cooperative. The belief was, if we could get something in place before more shares were sold, we wouldn't have to deal with a bunch of ideas from new shareholders.

The group nominated two people to go to the trust with our bylaws and find out if a trustee could figure out a way to work around our draft copy of bylaws. Our meetings started to pick up again where we tried to figure out the best course of action. Our members came back and said that the trustee wanted a study to be done on the land. These tests included perk tests and a test on environmental impact. During the next meeting, we were all informed that our two members had signed a legal piece of paper with the trustee to begin a study on the land. However, one of these people who signed the piece of paper wasn't even a shareholder. This is what had started the pathway to destroying our dream of a cooperative lifestyle.

Then our worst nightmares came true; the two shares were sold to off-islanders. It wasn't long afterward that rumors of Mill

Farm started flowing. We heard that the new owners began seeing a lawyer. You have to understand that most of the shareholders never even met these two new shareholders. I heard that one of the shareholders was a psychiatrist from Buddha knows where. They didn't even mind throwing a wrench into our family cooperative by going to a lawyer and threatening a lawsuit against any of the owners that didn't see things their way. Who cared if he was a nut doctor? That didn't give him more preference over us just because he thought he cornered the market on crazy. That psycho guy had no idea of how off-the-wall and stuck in a time warp some of the other shareholders that he had just partnered with could be. When we approached the Capital Regional District (CRD) for assistance, we were informed that the two new owners had already hired an individual to draft a bylaw based on the development and not on the holistic living and conservation.

Our paranoia about the worst potential Mill Farm disaster had just came true. A new member of the group had threatened a lawsuit against us because we wouldn't sign the draft agreement with the Islands Trust. One must understand that these new shareholders who bought into a cooperative had never even met many of us.

My wife and I realized shortly that we were the only holdouts on this new development. We stood firm and wouldn't sign the papers. The new owners were told that I was "a stick in the mud, old bugger" and that I would never budge. My partners told him that there was no way that I would ever sign anything that related to white triangular survey stakes being put into the ground. My wife and I wanted to stand by our original agreement of protecting the land from any development. After being threatened and abused over the years, Kimi and I had decided to stand Terra Firms on this incredible piece of earth.

One of the shareholders put the death sentence on himself when he said he would kill anyone that started legal action against the farm.

This shareholder came up to my house and said, "What's all this about threats? I certainly haven't threatened you and Kimi. What do you mean threatened? Actually, did you realize, Bruce, that if one owner says anything, you, your wife, your son Orin, [as well as] Sarah and your granddaughter will have to move off the farm? It's called the Practitioners Act: if one person wants to sell, that is what the courts do; it's like a divorce."

"Take your Partitions Act and shove it," I said.

"You and your group would be tied up in court for years. Don't you realize that it can happen if you don't sign the zoning bylaw?" he said as he pulled his suspenders in frustration. The gigantic, overworked elastic straps held up his huge jeans, which hid his short, squat body. I just watched the red flush of rage quickly overtake his round face, his plump cheeks aflame with rage.

My wife and I could see the gears in his head whirling around as he tried to find a way to convince the two most resistant co-op members to sign the papers. He turned himself around and lumbered across the sloping floor.

"We aren't signing nothing," I said as I gazed out of the glass wall to view Cowichan Bay, which was once one of the biggest estuaries on the west coast. What a sight indeed! The mud flats stretched along the shore, which was lined with enormous fir trees.

I turned around sharply. "I don't trust you and your new partners who want to sacrifice the land for dollars," I stated as my dark chestnut eyes bore holes through his being. He was livid, shouting loudly and carrying on as if it was unbelievable that Kimi and I couldn't trust him.

"I just don't understand this. How have I ever let you to not trust me?" he asked indignantly.

"Well, how about when we asked you to put the six issues in with the bylaws?" I angrily bellowed. "You agreed with those things and said you would sign them. It would be no problem since you have it on the computer and could add them easily. You never did that.

Talking about threats, how about when your partner told Kimi that we could lose everything we own, which was stated on September 20, 1994. How do you think that made my wife feel?" I said.

At a meeting, he agreed to put six of our concerns in the draft copy. Some of the points that we wanted to include were the original concepts of the Mill Farm bylaws, such as no survey stakes for land markings, no logging, and no subdivision. That was why I was so upset when he showed up on a mellow Sunday, foaming at the mouth about how we have been threatened. I was sick of being threatened by my partners in the Mill Farm. My family chose to follow the mandate of the Mill Farm with an alternate lifestyle.

I told my wife that if these threats kept coming, then all my gray hair that I'd grown over stressing about the Mill Farm would fall out. This was mental abuse. A person can't just come into someone else's house and expect you to trust him to be a good negotiator. That shareholder opened the floodgates of deception and then threatened my family and me with the Partition Act just because we didn't agree with his rezoning application that was filed at the Islands Trust Office. It was another subdivision file, based on greed. It seemed like he had no heart and didn't think of anyone beside himself. Please think about my side of the story for a minute. Look at what my family had at stake here. We had put twelve years of blood, sweat, and tears into the Mill Farm. How about the two million board feet of old growth timber that you swore would never be cut down?

Around this time, my family and I got off-the-wall comments and threats from others, even partners. Other shareholders who were friends started threatening us with the Practitioners Act. They told me that if we didn't sign the rezoning application, then we would lose our place on the mountain. Someone even phoned from Fulford Glass and threatened my son's girlfriend with losing their house on the mountain if we didn't sign the papers. One lady who had the three children sold her share and wrote a letter stating that she felt like she and her family were pushed off the land. This was a huge loss to our side when my son's girlfriend sold her share because she was the one shareholder who was supposed to be on our side.

I felt like I was being forced into a different mandate when complying with all the pleadings of the Partition Act violated my human rights. As a fact it was the first time in fourteen years of ownership history that everyone had agreed to the Partition Act besides my family and me. Then all of a sudden, two lawyers had a disagreement, and the petitioners changed their pleadings to an act that would put my family out of our homes. Should these people capitalize on our family's years of hard work, which included two houses and a shop as well as an incredible vegetable and flower garden? Was it really my family's fault that a lawyer legalized a letter of understanding by someone who wasn't a property owner in an important rezoning application? The constitution that was presented to the Islands Trust as a constituted set of bylaws were in fact not legalized at all but were just draft plans of a constitution. Owing to these acts, my family suffered hardship. If these were allowed to go through, everyone concerned, they would benefit even during this turmoil. A share sold for $85,000 in cash at fair market value. At that time, I felt that we had a lot at stake and had to ask that this matter go to trial.

Shortly after, we found out extremely disturbing news that some members attended a meeting with the new shareholders. My family and I were informed that they had approached the Islands Trust about gaining "special licensing status" because of the Partition Act situation. That day, a new bylaw was created where each interested party was at liberty to log or develop their own parcel of land as they wished. Two members of the group were selected to further investigate this situation with the Islands Trust. For a while, we had two different constitutions and bylaws governing the cooperative.

Life got really overwhelming. I thought about the uncertainty surrounding my family's home on the Mill Farm, which was too much to handle that my company started to go down hill big-time. I was emotionally drained after finding out about the new bylaws, which had been created, behind closed doors, to allow for the development of ten homes and ten guest cottages on the Mill Farm property.

You might wonder why this became a big controversy. After all, the original mandate stated that each one-tenth share was entitled to a family home. So what's the big deal, you may ask? A few guest cottages? Who cares? Well, it was a *big* problem. The covenant agreement, as it originally was drafted, stated no septic, no hydro, and no paved roads.

The new bylaw insisted that the development be up to current Capital Regional District (CRD) building and development standards. This meant white survey stakes, permits, twenty septic systems, hydro poles, and paved roads. Not to mention a public trail that was to be established in the northeast corner of Mill Farm. All of this was done without any studies whatsoever, period. Before any piece of land was divided you had to do a percolation test for septic tanks where most building sites were situated on solid rock. There was no way that there could be a septic drain field put on the majority of the sites. The new bylaw was created without any environmental assessment, geological surveys, or consultation with the property owners. The government survey stated that people were not safe to explore the area where the supposed trail would be located. Any questions we had were answered with the threat of legal action. No answers, just threats.

While working through the Islands Trust nightmare, four more shares changed hands. This time, two off-islanders bought the shares and accepted the terms of the covenant as originally drafted. We were quite relieved and everything seemed just as we thought it should be. Sadly, those feeling were short-lived. After the shares changed hands and before the ink was dry, the new owners served us with an order under the British Columbia Partition Act. It didn't take long for us to figure out what just had happened: we had been duped! Sure, the new owners were on board, but just long enough to lull us into a false sense of security and make us believe that my family's home was safe.

Then a glimpse of hope shone through the storm clouds. A friend who was more like a family member had won an insurance claim from ICBC for a lot of money. He won the claim because he became a paraplegic after an automobile accident on Salt Spring Island. He moved an old Airstream trailer over the mountain, and you would not believe how determined this young man was to fulfill his dream of living on the Mill Farm.

He bought a share from our partners who were working on the court documents with us. This share used to be our friend's parents' share in the Mill Farm Cooperative. Our partners who were on our side happened to see the writing on the wall, so to speak, and decided to sell their share to our friend and get out of the co-operative before the proverbial crap hit the fan. It was a blow for us to lose them, but our old friend was even more on our side in many ways and bought the share thinking he could help save the Mill Farm. It felt really good to have him on the hill at the farm.

It was truly amazing what our friend accomplished as a paraplegic; the drive over the mountain was difficult enough already. I wish to omit the name of my friend for a very good reason, as the reader will learn later on in the story. Once he made it over the hill to the entrance of the Mill Farm it got very rough. The municipal road was bad enough, but when he got to his driveway, it became very tricky to maneuver. He had to drive up a very steep logging road that most people had to use a four-wheel drive truck to get up. He drove a two-wheel drive van with hand controls over boulders and huge tree roots sticking out of the ground and just before he got to his place, there was a very steep incline, with loose rocks and boulders everywhere that would spit out from his front tires like missiles. They would strike the undercarriage with a velocity that caused dents and scrapes, making his new van look like a derelict vehicle before it even had a thousand kilometers on it.

Once at his place, he would go from his van into his trailer, which was totally gutted, using a hydraulic lift he had installed in the van. There was no heat, nothing at all in the trailer but a bed in the back; that is how determined he was to live over the hill. It was always exciting when our friend was around; I still remember many stories before he was a paraplegic. For instance, he was always really determined to make it up our driveway in a two-wheel drive vehicle. One night we awoke to a loud crashing sound. At the bottom of our driveway I had a pole structure for a shop that was all framed up, including roof rafters, and was ready for sheathing.

When you came up our driveway, which was basically an old logging road that was a stream of water in the winter, you had to go straight, make a very sharp turn to the right and then continue straight up to our house. He was going so fast when he hit the corner that the car wouldn't turn and he drove straight into my framed-up shop, bringing it all down around "the car of destruction," as I then called it. The amazing thing was that the car was not touched in any way whatsoever. By the time I got up and dressed to go and find out what all the noise was about, he had reversed out of the rubble and was backing his van down the driveway to give it another run, as if nothing happened.

He finally made it up the driveway in his van one night after my son's and his graduation in 1989. This is how our cast iron bathtub made it up the mountain. He loaded it onto the back of his van for weight, took a huge run at it and actually made it to the top of our driveway. His wish had finally come to a conclusion, thank goodness, fulfilling his dream of making it with a two-wheel drive. Yes, you guessed it, he was the only one ever to make it in a two-wheel drive vehicle.

I still miss my old Stihl 028 chainsaw; I had lent it to my friend back then. By this time, his van had no front windshield at all. Luckily, Salt Spring was pretty laid back at that time and you could get away with stuff like that. I remember not having new plates on my old International for eight years, although I would only drive it on the south end of the island and over the mountain. Back to the chainsaw story. For some reason he wanted a skylight in the roof of his van. He picked six o'clock in the morning in Mouat's parking lot. Picture this guy firing my chainsaw up and cutting a big hole in the roof of his van. No way, you might think, but yes, he did it, to the demise of my chainsaw.

I took that saw to our local Mr. Fix It, from the south end of Salt Spring Island. Whenever I saw him, I would ask him if it was ready.

"Oh yeah, it is high on my list, any day now," he would tell me. Over twenty years later, whenever I see him, I still ask him. The funny thing is I told a friend about it and he said his dad gave Mr. Fix It a Stihl chainsaw to fix, many years before I ever gave him mine to fix. Some call it island time. It sure makes for a good story anyway. I know Mr. Fix It, who we all love dearly, and there are a few more of these stories out there. We would always kid around that he was saving things to do in his retirement.

Things were getting pretty intense in the fall of 1995. People were getting afraid that if we lost the lawsuit, the Mill Farm would be bought by a logging company. It was a strange concept, when you think about it. The very people who wanted to change their whole lifestyle to save the farm years prior were the very same people who were now willing to change their lifestyle all over again for the "root of all evil," as my grandmother would call the almighty dollar.

There was a group of people who were working with the Pacific Conservancy organization to raise funds to buy the Mill Farm, in order to preserve it as a Provincial Park. Local artists, Carole Evans, who is an old friend of mine, and Carol Haigh, a friend of Kimi's, coupled with other artists, such as Robert Bateman, Brian Brett, Susan Musgrave, and Steven Reid, who all helped raise money. There were also many others who donated paintings, books, and their art to be auctioned off so that the proceeds would be added to the Pacific Conservancy Trust Fund to help buy the Mill Farm after the court case, if we lost the lawsuit.

It was becoming pretty evident at that time, after the research we had been doing and what people had told us, coupled with the fact that we did get advice from a local lawyer, that we were going to lose, and that it was a huge gamble.

GAMBLING FAMILY

I came from a gambling family. My old uncle Bart used to gamble huge; he even once won a hotel in Alberta in the early '50s by winning a poker game. I started playing poker for nickels and dimes in Bowness when I was just ten years old. I learned the game as a young man and played whenever they needed a fourth person to make a game happen when we lived back in the hills west of Nanton, Alberta. When I left home at the age of fifteen, my grandma said the best education I could get was to travel and talk with the old people I met.

At fifteen, I was quite a big boy and could easily pass for sixteen years old. In those days all you needed was a pink card to work. You would go to the unemployment office and tell them your name and birth date, then they would give you a pink employment card right there on the spot, without having to show any ID whatsoever.

At that time, in 1962, there were a lot of jobs available, and I got a job right away working in a road construction camp in Nordegg, building a new road at that time that ended at Nordegg.

I remember in the café they would be playing "Silver Threads and Golden Needles," over and over again on the jukebox.

The camps in those days were something else, just wall tents on platforms; the kitchen wasn't much to write home about, either. The cook went mad for some reason and went on a pork chop spree; all he would feed us was pork chops for days on end. We stayed in a wall tent with an oil stove in it for heat. Man, was it cold some days back in the mountains. One morning we all woke up cold, and all you could see were sets of white teeth shining in the blackness. The coal oil stove had gone out in the night, and everything—and I mean everything—was covered in a layer of pitch-black soot. There were no unions or laws of any kind protecting the worker at that time, so we had to put up with whatever they gave us to stay in.

There was one guy in our camp who had a story about how he sold a racehorse in Calgary twice in one day to two different people. We all thought, *Yeah, right,* at the time. Then one day a pickup truck showed up in camp asking about Johnny So-and-So. We never thought anything of it and told them where he was working. We did think it was strange that these two men were walking with him squished between their two hulking frames. Neither the company nor we ever heard from Johnny again. I guess his story was true, that he sold that a horse to two different people on the same day.

Every night after work, there would be a Stook game, which was very popular on the prairies at that time. Our boss, George, was the main man and always made sure the game was on. In those days you had to be very careful when playing cards. We caught one guy who was marking cards; the older guys worked him over real good, took his bank roll, divided it among all the regular players, and then ran him out of camp.

When winter break-up came, we headed into Red Deer, Alberta, where our company, Lindsey Construction, had their head office, in order to pick up our pay checks. I always felt sorry for this one young man who was working to go to school that fall. He had to sign his whole paycheck over to a guy because he had lost it all playing poker.

George had a room at the Arlington Hotel, where the poker game went on as long as we could stay awake. He said one day that he had to go home to Biggar, Saskatchewan, and asked if I wanted to come. He said he would show me all the gambling places and teach me the ropes. At fifteen I was full of adventure and said, "Sure!" Little did I know what was in store for me. First off, we went to Edmonton, Alberta, where he rented a room and the card game was on, but we lost all our money in no time.

He said, "No problem. I know a way to get more." I was all ears at fifteen years old; I had no idea what I was getting myself into.

Remember how I told you about the pink cards? Well, George told me to go down to the unemployment office and get a card under a fake name, so off I went and without any trouble got the card and went back to the hotel. I always wondered what was in that case George carried with him. It turned out it was a check-perforating machine, the ones you put a check in and it would come out all typed-up and perforated, looking very professional. I would hear him on the phone talking to some plumbing company, saying that he was from Revenue Canada and wanted to check their books. This guy was pretty smooth and said, "Before I come see you, I just want to check your bank account." They would tell him everything without thinking twice. Once he had all that information, he would write out a check to me under a phony name and it was off to the bank I would go. He had connections to all the different banks in Edmonton and made sure I would go to the one across town from where the company had their account.

Wages in those days were around forty dollars per week. He would make sure it was the beginning or the middle of the month and make it out for around sixty-nine dollars, which was a lot of money at the time. I would go into the bank and give them the check. It was so easy. All they did was ask me for ID, I would give them the pink card and then they would phone the other branch and soon enough the money would be in my hand.

Once we had the money, we went to the train station and bought tickets to Saskatoon. This is where I saw my first poker room. Under the local grocery store was a big room with low hanging lights and tables covered in green cloth. We did all right in Saskatoon and left to go to Biggar, Saskatchewan. I will always remember the sign when coming into Biggar that stated, "New York is big but this is Biggar."

If I remember right, the poker room was under the hardware store in Biggar. The players were all the town fathers, policemen, the mayor, and the owners of other businesses. These poker dens were everywhere in those days before casinos; some were even in the back rooms of local fire departments.

The next year, Lindsey Construction called me back and our first job was near Leduc, Alberta. I had just turned sixteen at the time. I was still at a very influential age and when I had alcohol in me who knew what kind of trouble I could get into. I feel a need to tell this story, so that the reader will understand why I came to the conclusion of my decision regarding the Mill Farm and why I chose to stick to my word.

It was a Saturday night, and we went into town. There were several of us. Wayne was over twenty-one and that was the legal drinking age at that time in most of the Canadian provinces. The first thing we did was pull up to a bar, and Wayne went in to buy some beer over the counter. We drove around Leduc and managed to pick up two local girls. This was the thing to do in Alberta in those days, drive around the country, drinking beer. After we dropped the girls off, we realized that we had no money and needed gas to make it back to the camp.

Wayne had this idea of his to get money that would end up being a life-changing experience for me. His plan was that he would go into the hotel, where by this time the beer parlor had been closed and the hotel clerk was cleaning it up. While he was talking to the night clerk in the bar, Doug and I would go into the hotel lobby, take the cash register and run out the door into the waiting getaway car.

I remember as I write this that there were four of us on that fateful night. Everything was going according to plan: Doug and I grabbed the cash register, ran out to the street to hop into the car with Wayne, but there was neither car nor driver there, to our surprise. So we started carrying that cash register toward the edge of town, heading for the nearby bushes about a half mile away in the northern direction. Once inside the bush, we started trying to open the cash register, which was much harder than you could imagine. With our hearts pumping like steam engines, we finally managed to smash it open. All there was inside was a couple of two-dollar bills, which were as rare as hen's teeth in Alberta. We stuffed them into our socks and started heading toward camp on the highway toward Calmar.

It seemed like we walked all night. We finally made it to camp and had just gotten into bed when dawn broke into a new morning. Along with the new light of day, the police were there, shaking us awake. It didn't take us long to figure out that the driver of the Packard getaway car ratted us out. Wayne, the older guy, was in jail and charged with contributing alcohol to minors, robbery, and some other charges. The cops lectured us up and down about how lucky we were that we were under eighteen. They told us that the town fathers didn't appreciate the likes of us courting their daughters and making trouble and that they would make an example of us. It was off to the big house for us, Fort Saskatchewan Penitentiary.

We were put in cellblock D, away from the getaway car driver because they were afraid we would do him harm. They kept us in there for three weeks in a cell by ourselves where you were only let out of your cell for exercise, one hour a day. Other than that you were shut in a tiny little cell for twenty-three hours a day. This was a huge wake-up call for me. I said to myself, *Once I get out of here, I will never do another bad thing ever again.* When our three weeks were up, we went to court in Leduc. We had already been told that Wayne had received two years less one day in a Provincial jail. Man, this scared me big-time, along with thinking about my grandma, who I never wanted to feel hurt by my actions.

Our boss was at the trial in Leduc, Alberta. Yes, the real crook, George the smooth talker, was going to smooth talk for us. We ended up getting one year of probation and were released into Lindsey Construction's care, so to speak. I was just happy to be free from that hellhole called "jail." Never again would I ever do any wrong. The one positive thing about being in jail at exercise time was that we would play poker for cigarettes. Back then they would give you a pouch of tobacco every week in jail. Along with the tobacco came a package of paper matches. To make them last, you would split them in half. For some reason I was a winner on the inside; I guess playing poker from a young age had its benefits. I always had a stash of cigarettes from winning poker so people never bothered me. I think they wanted to be friends with me so they could bum cigarettes.

TAX MAN

Meanwhile back at the Mill Farm Commune, the votes were cast; it was no surprise that nine of the ten shareholders were in favor of having the Mill Farm staked and paved. This is when the real harassment started with people trying to get us to agree to the subdivision. We were totally for going along with the original agreement and wanted to uphold the Mill Farm Constitution as it had been originally conceived. After numerous meetings intended to address the concerns of both sides, it became clear that an equitable resolution was going to be extremely difficult to achieve. When they decided to stop negotiations the law allowed them to take us to court. I was so stressed at this time it was almost impossible to run my glass company. One of my main objectives was completed, though: I always wanted to help my son get a trade, which I had fulfilled by having a glass shop and sending him to trade school. He ended up getting his journeyman's certificate. Thank goodness he got his certificate before the business started going sour, which happened in a hurry.

It really went downhill fast when a Ltd. Company in Victoria screwed me out of $90,000, which was a lot of dollars for a little company to absorb in 1993. I should have known when I went to see them in their office in Victoria. There was many different pictures hanging on the wall, and each one had a different company name on the bottom of it. I thought because the building was a government building I would be OK and believed him when he told me some kind of cock and bull story about how if I didn't put a lien on the building, my company would still get paid. Well, being a nice guy, I fell for it and said sure, I won't place a builder's lien on the building. Big mistake! It cost me $90,000, which led me into going broke.

Man, was I stressed out at this time. You could see my hair turning gray right before your eyes. Not one of my old friends had the gumption to come and visit us, to talk about this situation. I was "enemy number one," rightfully so, people thought, because it was I who was keeping them from making a lot of money. At this stage of the game, I had lost the company and was getting visits from the government. I was like a thorn in everyone's side. At the same time, it was the start of the famous GST. What a lot of people don't understand is that manufacturers in Canada paid a tax to the government for everything you bought. If I remember right, it was 9 percent manufacturer's tax. I still have a hard time talking about this; it was very hard having a business at this time. My whole life had just been turned upside down big-time.

The dealership that I had leased five trucks from was very good to me and just took the vehicles back. For some reason the government thought I was stashing dollars away and wanted to see where I lived. All of this made me feel like I had "wanted posters" out on me all over the island. They finally found me one day down in Fulford, driving some old wreck.

I told them, "Come on up to my house and see for yourself." The next day these two suits show up on the mountain at my door.

Well, it only took them two minutes to look around, and then they were bouncing down the driveway, which was really just an old cat trail that had been washed out over the years and was full of ruts and potholes.

All I really had to my name was the old fishing boat, *Miss Debbie,* I loved that boat, and for some reason they missed it. They pretty well took everything else. If I would have only known about how businesses filed for bankruptcy. My friend who was a supplier of mine went bankrupt to a tune of $43 million. That hurt me bad because I lost my number-one supplier and couldn't finish some jobs. He knew what he was doing and started a new company, which became one of the biggest in Vancouver.

I will tell you right here and now this is probably the number-one reason I would not sign the new by-law proposals. How could I when I was opposed in many different ways, when I deeply think about this peculiar situation? The funny thing was that a friend of mine was the head of the Islands Trust at the time. I knew for a fact that this was going to be this fantastic new development on a very isolated area on the slopes of Mount Sullivan, Salt Spring Island. Once it was done, someone who owned the next 160 acres could do the same thing. Especially since they were pushing it through with no environmental studies at all. This end of Salt Spring is different: it's not an uplift formation like most of the Gulf Islands that are composed of sandstone, like the north end of Salt Spring Island. There are cactus plants growing on a little island off Musgrave Landing. Most of the sandstone buildings in Victoria came from the Gulf Islands. What they would do is get one of those old wooden barges that was pulled by a tug. They would fight the currents of Collier Pass and pull the tug and barge up right beside the sandstone wall on Valdez Island. Boom, the dynamite would explode, bringing down the sandstone wall, loading the barge instantly, making it sit very low in the water. The TNT that helped harvest the sandstone was produced on James

Island. For many years, there was a CIL Explosives that had a huge place there, including housing. That is where they would make all kinds of explosives and gunpowder. In 1913 they established the dynamite plant on James Island. At its peak the plant employed eight hundred people. Most of whom lived in a small traffic-free village on the opposite end of the island. During World War II, the plant produced nine hundred tons of TNT per month. The TNT plant closed in 1977, and it and the village were disassembled and removed from the island in 1997.

The main reason there is no way I would want survey stakes on the mountain was that I heard our benefactor's brother say to her, "If I die, you will be the only beneficiary left to inherit the whole family estate, and I want you to do something good with the money." At the time our benefactor was quite the party girl in many ways, like snorting the white stuff up her nose. Not long after this, the brother died in a motorcycle accident and she inherited the rest of the family's estate. This is when she decided after many talks with everyone involved to buy the Mill Farm and sell shares to different individuals. I feel this is the number-one reason that I decided not to sign the new rezoning agreement, along with the fact that I told the spirits I would never put white survey stakes into the earth. I sat in on most of those early meetings, and I know that the land was bought to save it, not to divide it up, pave it, and sell it for a profit.

MISSION DREAM

I had a dream one night at this time after my granddaughter was born, and I was living through my heartfelt feelings again and being a clean vessel for spirit. I was babysitting one of the girls while they were down visiting their mom when I had this dream. I was a bit surprised to have this dream; deep in my soul I was afraid that I had done my loved ones on the other side wrong, by falling hard off the wagon.

My grandmother's voice gently vibrated through my heart. "I will always be here for you, my boy, never worry. I'm here at all times, no matter what anyone tells you, my boy."

The dream told me to go over to Mission outside of Vancouver. Then after getting there, I had to go outside Mission and take the first path to the left. It was very hard getting there with a thirteen-year-old girl. But I had to follow this dream, so I did, even though my wife seemed to be skeptical about my interpretation of having such a dream. My wife was a good friend with my last girlfriend who experienced a lot of my spiritual happenings, when she would stay over night in my bus. After a full day of hitching rides from

Tsawwassen Ferry terminal—back then I would ask for rides while I was on the ferry—we finally arrived at Mission. All the money I had left was just enough to buy a loaf of bread. After we walked along the road out of Mission for about a half hour, we came to a path through the trees. So we turned left and followed the path. There were blackberry bushes all over the place, and it did not look like a well-used trail at all. All of a sudden out of the darkness of the overgrown trail we broke into a brightly lit clearing with a group of people setting up a big, thirty-foot tepee. They came running up to us as if we just dropped down from the heavens.

A young man who later became one of my best friends told me an old woman wanted to meet me. She asked who I was. I told her and said that I used to be part of a medicine wheel and that I carried a pipe. I felt good talking about being a pipe carrier because I was clean and sober again. A lot of time when I used to travel around the country, old people would come up to me and look into my eyes. They would turn around and say to the people who would be standing around, "Yes, he is one of them." This happened to me often when we traveled around and asked the chief's permission to enter their territory.

The old woman told me something different when she looked into my eyes. She said, "You are an Indian." This I had never thought of before, was this the reason that I have always been accepted by Native people wherever I have traveled my whole life?

She said, "We have been praying for someone like you to come and help us. The first thing we need help with is to set that big tepee up."

I said, "Sure, I can do that for you, no problem." I learned that it was the first day that people were coming to set up the Elders Medicine Wheel gathering in Mission, BC. I had no idea what was in store for me at all.

Setting up a thirty-foot tepee is a hard job in many ways. You've got to set the poles up at the right length, otherwise when you put up the skin, it will end up too high off the ground or not high enough, and then it drags on the ground. The young men who were trying to set it up were having that exact problem. The first thing I did was to get everyone to form a little circle and have a prayer circle asking for help from the ones above.

I soon learned that the tattoo-covered people, with muscles popping and bulging out of everywhere possible on the human body, were from the local federal prison on day passes to help the Grand Mother. Thank goodness the poles were big, because to set up a big tepee of this size you need poles that are at least thirty-six feet long, and the bottoms of the poles were at least five inches thick at the base. I have been taught to lay the three main poles out on the ground and take the tepee skin out and spread it out along one of the poles. At that point when you are standing there, smiling and thinking how long should I allow for the stretching of the skin, you tie off your three tripod poles. Then you set the tripod poles up into the air, which was not easy for such a big tepee with heavy poles. With all the help we had, lifting the poles was easier than I thought. After the main three poles were up, we added the other poles, which I put underneath the main poles. Everything you do is done in a clockwise motion when setting up a tepee. I do everything in a clockwise motion, even when I go on a walk. After the poles are tied together they form a beautiful spiral shape. I should mention that we placed strips of material, which were the colors of the medicine wheel, in the east, south, west, and north.

Then we picked out the longest, thinnest pole that we could find. After laying it at the back of the poles, you tie the skin to it and pray that you tied it in the right place, for when you set it up, you have tied it at the right length. We raised the skin into position with it shaking as we let it fall into place, making the opening for the smoke to come out of. Once in place, we spread the tepee skin out. It all looked good when we spread it around the poles, except there was a fold in it that we just couldn't flip out so that it would all meet in an even placement around the poles. We tried and tried to flip the fold free many times. The last thing we wanted to do was take it down again after all the work getting it up there in the first place.

One of the young men said, "I can go up there and flip it free." I looked up and thought, *No way, it's thirty feet in the air.*

He said, "Don't worry, I can do it easy," so I said OK, go for it. Well, he grabbed onto one of the poles and climbed up it just like, for lack of a better term, a monkey. When he came close to the top where the poles are closer together he went from one pole to grabbing onto two of the poles. He rested for a second swinging many feet above the ground, suddenly he let one arm go and grabbed the skin, flipping it free from its fold. He slid down the pole in a split second with a huge smile on his face; the watching crowd broke out into awed applause. To my amazement the cover was perfect as we spread it around the poles and pegged the skin to the ground (by perfect, I mean it just touched the ground). All we had to do was straighten the poles out and, boom, it was good to go. The tepee had paintings of the eagle, wolf, bear, and other amazing pieces of art painted on it in bright colors. When we started a fire that night in it and looked at from the outside, the paintings came alive and danced to the flickering flames from the fire within.

People were arriving at a steady rate in masses early that evening. What a sight it was to see as everyone made his or her camps in a circle that had been marked out the day before. In the middle was the sacred fire pit, which would be started the next morning when the sun was just starting to rise over the Fraser River and the mountains beyond to the east. On the outside of the fire pit was a ring of rocks placed in a circle formation. There were bigger ones at every doorway in each direction, and in between were smaller rocks completing the circle. I learned that this was the second medicine wheel here. There were a lot of people who knew about this wheel. People were saying that there was close to six hundred people who arrived for the wheel.

I spent the whole day meeting people and helping out in any way that I could. They gave us the big tepee to sleep in. Kimi's daughter really seemed at odds about all of this, especially when the women started talking about a moon lodge. At first many women have a hard time when they realize that they need to go to the moon lodge if they are on their "moon" (monthly cycle). Well, guess what: it was my wife's daughter's first moon, and she just had turned twelve years old. A sister who I had heard about, who was the old woman's main helper and that ran the woman's sweat lodge, offered me tobacco if I would show the women how to build a moon lodge. It is basically the same principle as building a sweat lodge, but by using much longer willows that are tall enough to stand up in and leave a hole in the middle for smoke to go into the heavens above. It was a lot of fun helping them construct their moon lodge. After the structure was done the woman put their shawls and blankets over the willows and then covered them all with a tarp. On the floor they gathered up cedar branches and covered the floor with them. Wow, was it something inside—the aroma of the cedar hit you and after you got over the amazing scent, you opened your eyes to a beautiful bouquet of color as the woven shawls and designed blankets germinated in front of your eyes.

A few people had told me that the Grand Mother wanted me to sit in their council circle that evening. I was given a young man to be my helper for the weekend who would fill me in on the things I needed to know. There was also an area that was created for the children. The children's area had its own tepee and lots of arts and crafts supplies to keep them busy. I visited with people all day long that I had met before at gatherings or that we knew from friends in common.

Oh yeah—forgot about the cooking area. It was huge! The Grand Mother supplied everything: plates, pot, pans, and the food. You can imagine how major of an accomplishment this was. They had a main cook and a lot of people who volunteered for various things throughout the camp. There was a long list of people needed; the cook's helpers were the largest number on the list of volunteers.

Runners were sent telling people to come and be part of the circle of elders when the time came, and that time had come. I had no idea what was about to transpire at all. It was beyond my wildest dreams what came out of this circle. I soon learned that they called it the Elders Medicine Wheel and the elders involved were part of a board of directors that governed a lodge that was built on the Grand Mother's land near Chilliwack. A group of people did fund-raising and got enough donated funds to build a huge healing lodge on her property.

As I sat there in the circle, I realized I knew some of the people from prior ceremonies from years past before I fell off that proverbial wagon. There was the man we had a pipe ceremony with at the Stein Valley gathering in Lytton, bless him. Also the man I talked about that was just starting the journey that I met at the medicine wheel near Nakusp was there. He seemed to be partners with the woman who ran the ladies' sweat lodge. Also there was a couple from Keremeos I heard a lot about who had since moved down to the States. Like I said, I can't use names because most of the people I talk about are journeying on to the other side now, bless them dearly.

When it came my turn to say something in the circle, I sang a song that was given to me at the medicine wheel near Nakusp, which was actually closer to Edgewood when I think about it. It felt really good to sing this song because it is a cleansing song, and when I finished, the old man from the Lytton ceremony said he felt a strong presence when I sang it. I talked a bit about my past and how I became a pipe carrier. I told them that I was very tired and burned out for a few years after the trip north and that I had this dream and I had to follow it. The woman running the sweat lodge said she had heard a lot about me and tried to find my place on Salt Spring. She asked me about my place and I told her; she responded that, yes, that was the place she visited, but I wasn't home at the time. Her story was that she felt funny about stepping inside, but the door was open and she knew that someone spiritual lived there.

After everyone talked, the feather went to the Grand Mother. She said a few things about how the wheel was run; if anyone came to us to asking for healing, we were to tell her about it. There were to be no pipe ceremonies without her knowing. The people who wanted healing would be discussed at the evening circle unless it was an emergency, in which case the council would decide who would work on them.

After all this she said, "My prayers have been answered, and the Creator has brought this young man who is sitting over there." She nodded her head at me. "I was asking for someone to come who could run our healing sweats," she said with a grin, adding, "also to help set up tepees." I was biting my tongue because I couldn't speak as long as someone else had the feather. My head was spinning and my stomach churning, like a barrel rolling over the fast-moving rapids of a river gone wild. *How can I do this?* I wondered. *It has been like how many years since I was in a sweat?*

She could see the apprehension written all over my face and said, "Don't worry, son, we will all be at the sacred circle when you are having the sweat, and we will pray for you. Don't worry." It seemed to me my mind had already been made up before I could even speak. When it came my turn to speak again, the feather was passed to me. I said I would pray and do the best that I could. Soon I knew why she told that young man Joe to help me with whatever

I needed, as Joe became my fire keeper. As soon as the council circle was over, I wandered around the camp to find Joe. When I found him, we walked out back to the sweat lodge area. The women's lodge was already set up and a ways from it was another area all cleaned up, just waiting for a lodge. I offered Joe tobacco to be our fire keeper, along with prayers right away asking for help from the Creator and the spirits on the other side. In the morning we all met before sunup to start the sacred fire and do the morning prayers. The drumming and singing made my heart pound a beat of happiness as the sun arose for our first day of the medicine wheel. The Grand Mother would sing some welcoming songs along with the eagle song, and everyone would join in. A vibration of love went around the circle as each person looked to his heart side and introduced himself to the person standing beside him.

There were some stories told about how the wheel was going to go on for the next four days. Basically, it was everything that was discussed at the council circle the night before, such as who was in charge of what, who to ask about security, childcare, and that those on their moon should go and talk to the moon lodge. They weren't to be part of the circle if they were on their moon, because their medicine was too strong for them at that time. At the moon lodge there would be a lot of teachings about being a mother and caregiver. Grand Mother didn't want small kids in the circle and asked that people take their kids to the children's area where there would be a lot of activity for them in many different forms. Then she turned it over to the old man who told some stories about the medicine wheel and healing, along with some very funny stories to get people laughing.

Each doorway was prayed for in a sacred manner during this time, in order to welcome the spirits from each doorway to join us and make them feel welcome here. One of the first things is always to thank the old ones of the land for allowing us to be there. That is, of course, after you have thanked the Creator for this day and our lives and prayed to the Creator to come and give us help in healing ourselves from any sickness or disease that we might carry.

Then it was time for breakfast. All the spiritual helpers sat at one table, and you would just sit down and people would serve you after the prayer was said for the meal. Then when the helpers were served, everyone else started to serve themselves. At spiritual gatherings, servers and cooks never taste the food before it is prayed for. The breakfast was great; it included bacon and eggs, the whole deal. Everyone in camp was fed well always. There were plates made up for the moon lodge and taken over there right away after the prayers.

The Grand Mother went to the last medicine wheel at Edgewood. It was the last because a rainbow couple was using the sweat lodge for practices other than a sacred sweat. Once the old man from Keremeos heard about it, he said he was closing that medicine wheel down. He had the authority to do so because it was on his traditional territory, so he got a hold of the main guy who ran the Edgewood Medicine Wheel and told him no more. Well, when the old Grand Mother went home, she started having visions of having a medicine wheel in Mission, and along with the vision came the colors of the medicine wheel. So she went to the Stolo Nation and got permission to have it on their grounds. One of the first things she did was plant four cedar trees, one in each direction, and they stood just outside the large circle of stones that formed the wheel. Just thought I would tell you how this wheel got started, and the reason that I missed that last Edgewood Wheel was because I was prospecting up in the north.

Anyway, I went to the Grand Mother and told her about the people asking for a healing sweat. She asked me what they said, especially regarding what kind of healing they needed.

She said, "Just wait and see; you have to get the lodge up first," which we were doing at the time. We made the holes for the willows, praying for each willow and offering tobacco in the hole just before the willow was placed into it. Once the willows were up, bent over, and lashed together, we covered the lodge in blankets and a huge, heavy, old canvas tarp. The boys made a door out of some old sleeping bags. Now the big test was to have someone go inside and make sure that there was no light at all. Once that was done, along with all the prayers and the prayer mound, the sweat was ready, just before lunchtime. The Grand Mother came over right away for her inspection of the lodge; she liked it very much, offered some prayers, and sang a song.

Then things really got exciting. My uncle who gave me the golden eagle head to carry at the Edgewood Medicine Wheel showed up on the grounds. I was amazed at how the universe worked. Then I started beating myself up, thinking how can I possibly be running a sweat lodge, especially since my uncle showed up. Uncle assured me that all was good; the spirits worked in ways that are meant to be. I asked the Grand Mother if it was all right for Uncle to come in, and she said sure. She introduced me to a man who worked in Aboriginal Programs for Corrections Canada, along with a chief of one of the local reserves. She told me that I was going to give them a healing sweat. She then told me what they were asking for to be healed in a healing sweat.

The time had come to start the fire for the healing sweat. I was taught that it was good for people to be there at the start so that they can pray with the grandfathers before they are set upon the log platform. Each grandfather lava rock is held and offered tobacco as it is placed on the fire. We were using twenty-eight grandfathers for this sweat lodge ceremony. You start by offering the first stone in the middle. This one represents the Creator, then one in each direction starting with the east which is the earth, eagle, and physical aspects; then the south, which is the air, wolf, and mental aspects; west, which is the water, bear, and the emotional side of life; and finally north, which is the buffalo and the spiritual side of life. You make sure that you pray for everything, and the same things that the brothers are praying for. There were only four of us there; in the lodge she wanted the two men to have privacy. I was sure happy to have my uncle with me in the lodge. I remembered the story of my old friend from Alaska, always sitting in the northern doorway, which I did. There are four rounds to a sweat lodge ceremony, with the door being opened between each direction. The idea is to go through the lodge and leave everything inside with the grandfather rocks. For the first three rounds you pray for everyone in creation, and the last round is for yourself. You leave everything behind, and then when the fourth door opens, you crawl past the grandfather rocks, thank them, and leave all your physical, mental, emotional, and spiritual wrongdoings with them. Then, you go out into the world as a new person, leaving all your baggage behind in the lodge.

In each doorway there are teachings to help people with healing themselves. If something happened during your life when you were say, sixteen years of age, you would be asked to sit in the southern doorway where prayers were said and songs sang to help you get past the traumas of the past. Many people have burdens put on them when they aren't even theirs to carry. Residential school comes to mind, how children and grandchildren carry things that are put on them by relatives that went to those schools. Many generations have been affected this way, even though they never went to the schools themselves. The affects of those schools are so ingrained in some people that they have stuff put on them without realizing it. Survivors put their own traumas of the past upon their children and grandchildren without even realizing what they are doing. What people need to understand is that they are giving their perpetrators power by even talking about what happened to them. I think that is why I was asked to run the sweat lodges; the Grand Mother had heard good things about me through the "moccasin telegraph."

We had a very good sweat, and when we came out of the lodge many hugs went around and thanks was given to the fire keeper who looked after the fire and the doorway. When we entered the lodge, everyone was sitting in their spots. Before the lodge, we had talked with the participants, and we knew what they were asking to be healed from in the lodge. They all sat in the appropriate doorway for the required healing needed. Once everyone was inside, the fire keeper passed all the medicines, drums, and water into the inside of the lodge. He waited until the sweat lodge keeper asked for grandfathers when again prayers were offered and the medicine for that doorway was offered to the red-hot grandfathers. The first round in the lodge I ran began at the eastern door. Each door has seven grandfathers come in through it, one at a time. They are brought in when asked for with a long tin pitchfork. The fire keeper has a helper also that sweeps the ash off the grandfather before it enters, keeping all ash and embers outside. The last thing you want in the lodge is an ash-covered rock, because when water is offered to them, they give off smoke inside instead of clean steam for your lungs. The medicine for the eastern doorway is tobacco. Along with many prayers, we really try to always use the sacred tobacco that was offered to us along with some natural tobacco. We were taught when the tobacco is offered to the grandfathers, the smoke from the tobacco carries our prayers to the Creator. Every grandfather rock is offered prayers and tobacco, and once that is done, we offer more prayers and splashes of water to the rocks. The steam gets very hot, and you have to be careful when you are the bucket man not to burn yourself and others. Over the years I have used buffalo horns to scoop the water up, but I have come to like a few cedar boughs tied together to splash the grandfather stones. Before I forget, there is also a set of deer antlers to bring the grandfather rocks in off the fork and place them in the pit in the middle of the lodge.

A hole was dug and prayed over before the willow frame was erected. It was about six inches deep and clean of all organic matter. The earth from the pit was moved out to the front of the door to make the prayer mound, where all sacred objects including pipes were placed. Some people had a pipe ceremony inside the lodge before the sweat ceremony. In some people's teachings, it was always a pipe ceremony first, but at this gathering the Grand Mother says no pipes. The old girl had her vision of the wheel, so we didn't question her wants.

Once the seven grandfathers are prayed over, the tobacco is offered and water splashed on each one, then you call for the door to be shut. The fire keeper lets the door shut which is rolled up onto the roof of the lodge. Before the ceremony starts, you ask the participants if there is anything they need to be blessed, if they have something like a new drum for example, or a ceremonial dress that is going to be used that year. They are invited to put these items on the roof of the lodge to have the energy and the prayers of the lodge go into them. Once the door is shut and the corners are all tucked in so as no light comes in, the sweat lodge ceremony starts. The fire keeper sits outside the door, not letting anyone interrupt our ceremony. It gets very hot inside, especially when water is splashed on the grandfathers. I have a teaching where you have to offer to the grandfathers the whole bucket of water that comes in the door every round. You don't want to burn anyone, so you are very conscious of this fact. It is not an endurance test to see how hot you can take in the hot steam, so if you get too hot, you can call out, "All my relations," and the fire keeper opens the door fast. That is what we call out at the end of each round, after we have prayed for all the women and caregivers that sit in this first doorway, along with our hearts, the eagle, the Mother Earth, and the mineral kingdom, to name a few. At the end after all the people have said their prayers, we all holler at once, "All my relations!" to open the door. Everyone crawls out of the lodge in a clockwise manner, sometimes it is all you can do to make it outside the lodge and lay on the cool earth, because you are so hot. After a little talking and a smoke break for some, we enter the lodge again for the southern doorway. Once everyone is inside, seven more grandfathers are added to the other seven. It is getting hotter every round, and the fire keeper always makes sure that the grandfathers are covered with burning wood, which in turn keeps them red hot. In the southern door we offer sage, which takes away all negative energy. The southern door is for grandfathers, fathers, sons, and uncles, and for all the male energy. We have a teaching that the bowl of the pipe represents the female energy in the eastern door, the beginning, and then in the southern door is the pipe stem representing the air and the male energy.

When I do wedding ceremonies it was always a good teaching that when you bring the bowl of the pipe together with the stem it represents the coming together of a couple, united as one. The southern doorway is where the family sits, along with the feeling of patience. I was told many years ago that all people were a circle of one, which broke apart into tribes, clans, and families, and now we stand alone in the middle. We need to bend over and help the missing links get back into the circle. At that time all races were given an element, color, and a gift to share in the circle. We will never have peace in this time until all races sit in the circle and share their gifts. Since I have entered the northern doorway, I have been told to write this down, that we need to share and speak our truth in a circle of one, and also that I need to write my spiritual name down, Chanukah Methionine, which means good spirit walking. One of the teachings of the northern doorway (spiritual door) is change. In the east, the Creator of us all gave the red race the element of the earth and the gift of vision; in the south, the yellow race air and the gift of patience; in the west, the black race the element of water and the gift of strength; and in the north, the white race the element of fire and the gift of motion. Each race of people needs to learn from its gifts and to sit in a circle of one and share its gifts in this time, so that our children will have peace in their lives.

I often think of the southern doorway and the yellow race and think about patience, to learn to have patience. I think about the yellow race living with so many people in their region; if they can do that, certainly I can have patience for what I need. While we were having the sweat, there was a main circle going on around the sacred fire. All the people would be praying for us in the lodge. This became very evident when I was running the healing sweat the next year at the Elders Medicine Wheel.

Grandmother Grizzly wanted to get a young man's attention in the sweat lodge, as he was sitting in the western doorway of the bear. In the darkness we heard a scream when we were praying for the man.

He hollered, "All my relations," got up, and out the door he went. When the young man went outside and stood up, people's mouths went huge and agape. The young man had scratches that were bleeding all the way down his back. He was really freaking out and said no way was he going back into the lodge. I calmed him down, saying that the spirits wanted to get his attention about what he was praying for. The best medicine for him was to go back into the lodge and pray hard; after all, it was his prayers that brought the spirit into the lodge. He went back into the lodge for the last round. I told people to go into the fetal position and prepare themselves to be reborn into a new day by leaving the yesterdays behind. When the round finished and we heard, "All my relations," the door opened, and as the young man crawled out we could see that there wasn't a mark on his back at all. The power of prayer is a very strong healer in many different ways.

It was suppertime when we finished up with the sweat. The best thing I liked about the supper was that the women always made lots of huckleberry pies, mainly because one elder loved huckleberry pie and, yes, ice cream as well. The talk around the table was always a lot of fun. It was great getting to know everyone, and there was no lack of stories. One of the main ones was about a woman who came to the wheel in a wheelchair. They had her in the main circle, which became a healing circle on many occasions. Everyone prays for the person in the circle and sends them positive energy, and the old Grand Mother lays hands on them. After the Grand Mother laid hands on her and prayed, the woman just got up and walked. She was wheelchair bound for years, but no more.

At the council that night, they told me they wanted me to say something in the circle the next day.

The next day, I told the story about how I found my friend Milton when I left my friend with the fire burning on Salt Spring Island. I felt I needed to share this story about Milton's friend who lived in the house where we had the sweat. He had one of the best raven stories ever. He was working on Salt Spring many years ago and was sitting on the ocean having lunch when a raven hopped by, dragging one wing on the ground. The raven started going into the bush, so he followed him. The raven jumped up into a tree, and my friend climbed after him, thinking he could catch the raven. I don't want to say his name because I want his spirit to travel freely to the other side, and I don't want him to think I'm holding him back. Then the raven flew away, and on the ground were some old moss-covered planks. When he lifted them, there was an old well. He got the water sampled at the University of British Columbia, and they were amazed that it was the most mineral-rich water they had ever seen. He was invited to one of the first potlatch ceremonies in Tofino, BC, after Native people were allowed to conduct their potlatch ceremonies again after it being against the law for many years. When he was there, he told the raven story to a group of old people. When he finished, they asked him if there were three islands to the south, and he said yes.

They chatted among themselves and said, "We think you and the raven have found our lost ceremonial water well that we have only heard about in legends." I told this story along with some about the Edgewood Medicine Wheel, so that the people would know my background story.

The final day of the wheel was coming up. Everyone was so at peace, it was like coming home to be with all these lovely people. The closing ceremonies were like a giveaway; everyone got an honorarium, which came as a shock to me. It included an envelope with cash in it, plus many gifts. My sister and I received blankets to carry the medicine wheel teachings on; they were real nice handmade, woolen blankets. One of the main teachings of the wheel is to set a stone down in the wheel. You remember where you put it on the wheel for when you come back the next year so that you will be able to put your new rock ahead of the one you placed the year before in the circle of stones. It is really good to keep moving through the wheel of life. In other words, don't get stuck in a rut; keep moving forward in the wheel of life. I always break up the wheel into twenty-eight sections, so that each section is like two and a half years of your life.

The wheel was a really good tool to use for healing a person by helping him to leave things behind. We first figure out at what age the person was when the trauma happened. We would wrap that person in a buffalo robe and lay him in the wheel in the doorway that is appropriate for the time in his life that the trauma happened. People will work and pray over the person, and there is always one healer who sits close to the person, sharing many heartfelt feelings of healing with him. After everyone feels the person is ready, they help him stand and when he has his senses back again, they walk the person to the spot in the wheel where he is in life at this time.

When the Grand Mother was saying the closing prayers on a still day, all of a sudden a zephyr of wind came up and blew her hat off, blowing it very high into the sky. It was like saying see you later to your own family. People had become so close to one another. I forgot to tell you, there were even people from the gathering I attended in Idaho years earlier. My wife's daughter was so happy it was all over because she had to spend the whole time in the moon lodge. As we traveled back home to the mountain, she spoke of the things she had learned from all the old grandmothers about life and becoming a caregiver. After the gathering, all the women told the group that it ended up being one of the best experiences of their lives, and they hoped that they would be on their moon again when they visited the medicine wheel. Before I left, the Grand Mother made sure to give me her address and the times when they had circles at the healing lodge in the Fraser Valley.

MY REAL DAD

In my mind, right now, I'm working up to tell you the story about meeting my real dad for the first time in my life since I was nine months old. The first time I really thought about him was when I ran away, trying to find him. I was eight years old at the time, living in Bowness. I thought about who he was over the years and wondered who this man was. Throughout my life I was always deeply hurt because the man called my real father never once tried to see me or look me up at all. So when my old girlfriend and I were staying in Alberta, we went to the foothills near Nanton, Alberta, where I was raised on this amazing old homestead in the magnificent foothills. It was perched on a hill looking over Pine Coulee, where eagles, falcons, bears, and all types of wildlife made their home. I can still feel the wind whipping the back of my neck as a hawk dive-bombed us kids to keep us away from her nest, nestled in the crags of the protruding sandstone outcrops of the Coulee.

When we visited the old farmstead, the owners were more than welcoming to us. When I tried to tell them about my past, the man brought out a history book. My real dad's family was in it, and it said that he lived in Calgary with his family and worked for this oil company based in Calgary. After spending the night sleeping outside, looking out over what seemed like the entire world. On the hill where the house was built, where the old scout camp use to be, you can still see the tepee rings. You can see the curvature of the earth as the northern lights and stars outline your picture frame of dark-shaped foothills. On our way to Calgary, we stopped by where my old uncle Ted lived in an old granary. It stood there in more shambles than I remember as a young man, some thirty-five years earlier. I will never forget the image of the old man sitting there shelling peanuts, as I myself throw a peanut shell into the corner of my hut and place the unsalted nut between my smiling lips.

When we were going through Calgary, my old girlfriend said, "Let's find your real dad."

I said to her, "No way, you got to be crazy. He never once has tried to look me up before, so there is no way I'm going to look him up now even if he was standing right over there." She said that we had better stop to get some gas, because she needed to use the little girl's room. After the truck was filled with gas, I looked all over for my girlfriend, wondering where she had gone. This wasn't like her; she always just did her business and was back in the shotgun seat ready to roll. I pulled the truck over out of the gas lane and parked it to the side. I was just about ready to go and find her when I saw her coming out of the service entrance to the gas station with a big smile on her face.

As she got in the truck, she started talking right away.

"I did it." she said.

"Did what?" I asked.

"I can't believe that I found your dad!" she replied.

I felt a dagger going into my loving heart upon hearing these words. It made me automatically say, "No way, I don't want to see this man they call my 'real dad' period." As my partner, at the time she knew that it would be very healing for me to meet this man.

She said, "Well, it's up to you, but I think it would be the best thing for you to do. After all, I have his phone number and address. I was going to phone but thought that was being a bit pushy, and I wanted you to be the one to phone."

I asked her, "How did you do this?" with an enquiring look or what could better be called a scowl on my face.

"Well, when we looked at that history book, I remembered the name of the company he worked for. So I found the name and phoned, and they said he was retired and no longer there but was still in contact because one of his sons works there," she explained. She never did say what she told the secretary, but somehow I still don't know how she got my real dad's phone number. In today's world something like this would never happen. People were more trusting back then.

I was stuck between a rock and a hard place. How could I phone this man who had never given me the time of day? I thought about this as my girlfriend was telling me all the positive things about it, like I could ask are there any health issues that I should know about in my family, and that kind of stuff.

I said, "OK, OK, give me the number and I will phone." So I went inside and put a dime into the pay phone and dialed the number, written on a crumpled-up piece of cardboard. A pleasant-sounding woman answered the phone.

I said, "It's Bruce Williams calling," and she just started crying and I could hear the phone drop. I held a silent phone to my ear, wondering, *Now what?*

Then all of a sudden I heard her say, "It's your son, Bruce," and a soft voice came on the end.

"Yes?" the voice said.

I said, "It's Bruce Williams. I got your number, and we are in Calgary."

He sounded very nice and excited to see me and gave me his address. It was unreal. We were only about two miles away from where he lived.

When we arrived, needless to say I had beyond butterflies in my stomach; in fact, it felt more like wasps. The door opened and I was looking down at my real dad, who was only about five feet seven, which is short compared to me since I'm six feet tall. I couldn't see any resemblance at all.

He sensed it and said, "Just wait till you've met some of your half brothers." They seemed like very nice people and said that they always wondered if I would ever show up at their doorway. They invited us in for tea, and the next thing he said to me was, "Do you know that your mom was an Indian?" I will never forget that. In my later life I was starting to realize why a lot of things happened to me when I was younger, like when I was a young child going to school. I could never figure out why I was strapped the first day of school and bullied by all the boys. Also, friends growing up were the Indian foster kids and the one black youth in Bowness.

I became very comfortable in their home; you could tell they were very happy to see me. I was amazed to hear that I had a huge family I knew nothing about. He had been married a few times and had six sons, including me. He was now married to his current wife, and she had three children. They were like a couple of lovebirds who met in their later years. They wanted to call over some of my brothers, but I said no, this was enough for me to take in right now after all these years. We made plans that they would come out to the coast and visit during the next winter.

I felt totally rejuvenated after the medicine wheel. My faith in humankind had been renewed, and I was ready to work for the spirits again. It really helped me when I was going through all this legal stuff about the Mill Farm Cooperative. The threats and insults were mounting, which made my wife very edgy in many ways, especially when I was starting to follow my dreams again. Not many people can understand my faith in following my dreams. It is hard for a lot of people to understand these kinds of things where you just drop everything and go. After all, I'm no high school dropout, as you have probably figured out; I never even made it to high school.

When I got back up the mountain, it was really good to be able to take all my medicine out because the Grand Mother had given me permission to follow my teachings again since quitting marijuana and drinking. Just before I left, she gave me permission to run sweat lodges. This to me was a huge message that the two men we sweated must have liked the sweat lodge ceremony. At a later date I would learn just to what extent they liked my lodge, because of an honor that was offered to me.

CRYSTALS AND SPARROW HAWK

By this time I had lost my glass business and was very perplexed about our situation. I could even feel my family's energy; they were wondering if the old man had lost his mind. A friend of mine was building deck chairs and asked my son to make them for him, which he did. I was pleased my son got some work to do after the glass company shut down.

A friend who called himself Sparrow Hawk was really into crystals, and he started telling me a lot of things about them and other wild stuff. He wanted to be my apprentice to learn how I did spiritual things, especially after I held one of his crystals and it exploded in my hand. He went on and on about how something was in that crystal and that it had felt my energy and escaped. I took all this with a grain of salt, so to speak. He wanted me to take some crystals and copper pieces, and make healing tools out of them. I made one for myself. It was like a pendulum, and when I worked on people, the first thing I would do is place this pendulum crystal above them, and it was amazing what this crystal would do. It would go in all different directions every time when I held it above people, and it would tell me many things about what was wrong with them. It was a great tool because it showed people exactly which meridians it followed and needed help, healing certain organs.

I started telling Sparrow Hawk about what I did when I was on the road in the bus, healing people. I never talk about this normally because it has to come through spirit, and I thought it was meant to be that I tell this man. Especially after one day when I was working in his shop down near Fulford. When I smelled a spirit, it came in the form of an amazing chocolaty-almond smell. I silently thanked it for coming and told it I was here to help it, telling it my name and that it was OK and not to be afraid. When this happened, they only stayed around for a few seconds. To my surprise, Sparrow Hawk started going crazy, saying there was a spirit here and that it smelled like chocolate almonds. I was amazed he smelled it and recognized that it was a spirit. I took this as a message from the spirit that I should work more with this man, who also said we were brothers in a past life.

So I started telling him about my breath that the spirit gave me, and how I used that breath for everything, including healing in the sweat lodge ceremony. I also told him how I had taken bad energy out of people and that it was very important to keep that energy confined so that it didn't go into another person. He really wanted to learn about this and to take part in a ceremony doing this. I told him that I worked alone and have never had anyone help me because of the danger involved in taking on someone else's bad energy. At the time there was a lot of talk that what came into me down in Idaho was a Gray.

He tried every way possible to get me to let him work with me, but I kept saying no, it is something that came to me in spirit, and I follow spirit only and not the two-legged one. In fact my grandmother once told me when I was a young child, "My boy, don't follow the two-legged ones." At the time I thought she was talking about my friends who I hung out with. Back then I was in our little Snake gang in Bowness. The main reason we formed the gang was to play poker. Just kidding! In reality it was to be able to protect ourselves against the bad boys who were out to get us. I was going to say bullies again, which I said earlier, but just realized that there was no such term as "bullies," if I remember right, in 1953. I later realized that what she meant to tell me was to never get in between the Creator and another person. That it is, after all, one's personal journey to learn one's own evolution in this time that has been given to us. The best thing that I have come to terms with in this lifetime is that life is our karma's journey, not someone else's. I kept telling him no when he asked about the spiritual things that I had learned. It wasn't something at that time that you just started blabbing about, standing in the middle of Ganges at the local Saturday market.

The tools that we were making became marketable items, and a lot of people wanted to purchase them. He would take them to all the local weekend markets at the time. One thing I would do was put the different colors on them. I used the colors from the sweat lodge ceremony, which sat in the four main and cardinal directions. One of the main colors I used, which came to me from my spirit guides for protection, was purple. I did tell him how I carried a roll of colored cloth to form a protection ring around me during my work.

I would do my breathing everyday, sometimes all day long at this time. It didn't sit very well with my wife. She had heard about a lot of my spiritual happenings through her friend who was my old girlfriend. Now my wife was seeing it for herself how I had changed after I had quit drinking and followed that dream that took me and her daughter to Mission to the medicine wheel. One of my dear old friends did the same up on the mountain; she followed spirit and felt she carried the spirit guide of Merlin.

For many years I knew this woman as a friend, and we had worked together in a spiritual manner many times. So when she came up the mountain and started talking about all of this spiritual stuff, a lot of people called it "airy-fairy garbage" at the time. Most people thought those of us on Salt Spring were right out of our minds. Especially my old drinking buddies. They were always teasing me, so I just started avoiding them, particularly since they would always try to get me to go party with them.

Anyway, this woman asked me to do a healing on her, and at first I was very leery in many ways, but deep inside I wanted to try out my new protection method. Remember I said if I knew the breath that was given to me from the spirit in Idaho, then I think I could have helped the woman.

So I said to her, "OK, let's try. What we will do is push the spirit into me, then I will feel it and then push it back to you." She didn't want to lose the spirit that she felt was Merlin; she just wanted me to feel the energy. So we asked my wife if she would be the pusher of the spirit, and to my surprise she said yes. This was no joking matter in many different ways, and I really to this day don't know why, but I decided to do this crazy idea that my friend wanted.

So we prepared for this in our small mountain home overlooking Cowichan Bay. So I got my medicine bag out and started doing my prayers while I was setting out my medicines and my roll of protection. We did this standing up with me facing my friend and my wife standing behind her. I had to do my prayers and send my energy inside of her, with my healing breath. When the time was right my wife was to push on the middle of her back area, right opposite of her solar plexus area. When the time was right, I nodded at my wife, and she pushed the energy into me. My back was covered with purple material. Boom, the energy entered me, I felt it majorly and knew there was definitely an energy there big-time, who knows if it was Merlin or not. All I know is I felt energy. I just wanted to get it out of me, and as soon as she pushed on our friend's back, she went to my back and pushed. This was all planned out so that the energy wasn't in me for a long time. So as soon as my wife got to my back, after she placed a purple cloth upon our friend's back, she pushed on the middle of my back and instantly the energy left me as fast as it came. My friend was elated that she had her energy back, and I was amazed what had just happened to me. As I write this I can't believe I did this, I must have really been confident at the time; I had all the belief in the world. I was learning that all of this stuff required 100 percent no fear whatsoever, and you needed to have 100 percent *faith*, which I did, especially because of what was happening as a result of doing my daily prayers.

On the other side was Sparrow Hawk, always trying to get information from me, especially after I told him the story about what happened up the mountain. He really wanted to learn all this stuff, but I just couldn't do it, because the spirit needs to tell me before I can do anything. He offered me this smoky quartz and said it was a gateway crystal to the thirteenth dimension. At home I was constantly praying and breathing my breath. I would especially use my breath for healing myself. He told me to try it and hold it in when I did my prayers. Having to be quiet at home when my wife sleeps after her night shifts gave me plenty of time to do my meditations. So I started holding this crystal in my heart-side hand when I was breathing. It turned out to be amazing and my breathing exercises started to change right away. The first thing that started happening was that spirit said you have to clear your chasers out. I had no idea what was going on with chasers, but I was about to learn many things by listening, feeling, and absorbing everything that came to me. I had learned how to protect myself after the Gray came into me in Idaho. So the first thing I would do was put a ball of white light around myself for protection, which was working very well, along with a medicine bag that Milton's sister made especially for me for protection after I told her the Idaho story. It was a beautiful beaded leather medicine pouch with her medicine that she prayed over placed inside the bag. She told me to adjust the straps so that it sat right over my solar plexus area.

One of the first spirits that came to me was Jesus. I was totally amazed at what was happening to me during these meditation prayer sessions. When I said prayers, the first thing I would always do was to pray to the Creator first and foremost and ask for my grandmother and mother to come to me, along with all my spirit guides.

When Jesus came to me, he said that I needed to protect myself from all dimensions. He told me that how he left the cave before they opened the door on the third day was that he placed himself in a star tetrahedron. He said the ball of white light protection was good, but I needed to wrap myself in the ball of light and then envision a star tetrahedron. Once I envisioned the tetrahedron, I was to open the door and sit inside, encircled in my ball of white light. After this session I had to find a picture of a star tetrahedron, which was very hard to do at that time, when there was no Google. So I had to ask Sparrow Hawk, and he found a picture for me, which helped me a lot.

In my prayers I was also being guided as to how to clean my chasers and how to line them up by using certain colors. I shared some of this with my wife at the time, but she didn't seem too interested until she bought a book about light. The book had approximately the same colors that I told her the spirit shared with mw. I was told that I needed to start from the bottom and work up my chasers. It is like a tube that goes through from your bottom, the perineum, and goes to the top, the crown chakra. Visualize it as a wilted lily at the bottom and on the top and the in-between chasers have two wilted lilies, one in the front and one at the back. Use your breath and get right into the area, called the root chakra, where we carry all our mental, physical, emotional, and spiritual hurts and pains. You need to go in there and get rid of it all and open that lily up like a vibrant flower of life. At the bottom visualize that you are peeling an apple and taking off all the layers of trauma. While doing this visualize the color red. It is important to do this in sequence when opening these areas up. At first for weeks all I would get is the color black, until Jesus came to me in a white light form. When I was meditating a form came to me, a tall greenish-blue sort, that said he was made from electrons from Atlantis. He told me that huge crystal generators powered Atlantis. He said that in the fifth dimension there are nine chasers, that when going through your chasers, it is important to put two chasers out above your head one to each side; he said these are very important when you leave your body, but you still have a lot of work to do before this happens. Every day was very exciting to me in many ways at this time, which helped me a lot to take my mind away from what was happening with the Mill Farm Cooperative.

I would pray a lot every day, and every opportunity I got to be alone, I did my breathing and protection, working very hard on my chasers. It literally took me a few months to get by the first chakra. The positive thing in all this that kept me going is that I was starting to get color finally along with the dark blackness. The color that was starting to come was the color red; this amazed me because they said red was the root chakra color. I would keep cleaning it out with my breath and visualizations, while doing this I would clean and go around and around the flower that I visualized as a lily, and it was starting to open up. The feeling I was getting was that once this flower was wide open, I'd have finally got the job done and have swept all the corners clean. The time finally came when I went into my meditation and the color red would come right away. Now I could start working on my stomach area, which carries a lot of sickness in all aspects, which is also similar to the root chakra. The color you think of is orange and, yes, a good thing to do is visualize peeling an orange, which I did along with opening up the two lilies. For weeks on end this is what I did, and I went down the hill to make healing tools with Sparrow Hawk, who believed he was a reincarnation of Merlin. This is the main reason I told him about our exercise up the hill with my old friend and my wife.

One of the main reasons Sparrow Hawk wanted to do spiritual healing was because he had a friend in Vancouver who carried an entity for ten years and had gone to many healers to get help with it, but they always came to the same conclusion that they couldn't rid her of this energy. He even got her to write me a letter. Funny how when I'm writing this now how strange it seems to say she wrote me a letter. I had no phone and I have never really liked the phone—even sitting here now sharing this with you, I don't own a phone, and it wouldn't help anyway because where I live there is no service, period.

Her letter really got my attention when she talked about what she was going through and how her energy was coming to an end in this life. These energies that come into people do take away your life energies in many different ways. Some, like the one I had, seem to take your life force right out from under you, where others work at a much slower rate. I could go on, like my auntie, on this subject, but I need to get on with this story. I told Sparrow Hawk, "OK, I will help her, but by myself." He didn't like this and tried to come up with every possible excuse that I needed his help. I still told him no, that I needed to do this alone. So off to Vancouver we went to meet with this woman at her apartment down in the west end of the city. She lived in one of those old walk-up apartment blocks.

After meeting her I asked Sparrow Hawk to go down the block to a café and that I would come get him after we were finished. He did not like this, but it was what it was. I set up all my medicine and my protection circle. I always do my work with the person standing in an upright position. I also wear a vest that has the color purple and little round mirrors sewed into it. I pray a lot, sing a song welcoming the Creator, grandfathers, grandmothers, and spirit guides to come and help us. I did my breathing and went inside her with my energy and felt where she said it hurts. I knew it would be in the solar plexus area—seems this is where they all hang out, where our soul sits. When I'm inside, I'm telling the entity what I'm doing and who I am, just like it is sitting right in front of me, and at this time we would just give them back to the earth. After some time of doing this exercise over and over again and getting a good feel of what's going on, I stand at the back of the patient and push on this middle of the back in order to send the entity out. A lot of times you are asking your helpers to help them to the other side. Many spirits that have died violent deaths and have not had time to prepare for their next journey get caught up on this side.

Right away afterward she said she was feeling much better. I went out the door to get Sparrow Hawk. He was right outside her apartment door, waiting with anticipation. I told him it went all right, and we went back up to her place. She was so thankful, she said she felt better than she had in ten years and gave me a lot of gifts. On our way out the door, we said to make sure and keep in touch. With this being done, it meant she was finally ready to get married, which she never wanted to do as long as she felt that way. A few weeks later I got a letter from her, and she said that she felt so good that she finally accepted the wedding proposal and hoped we would come.

Man, this made Sparrow Hawk even more persuasive about trying to be my helper. He was just like some little kid always bugging you for candy or something; he was driving me crazy with his wants. He told me he would make a copper shield with protection crystals on it and hold it in front of me for protection. He came up with another long-winded story about this woman he met while selling crystals at a Sunday market on Government Street in Victoria. It was another case where she never knew what to do and Sparrow Hawk obviously knew how to get my attention by now. I felt a real connection to this man because of the crystal he gave me. Who knows if it did have powers or was it just my prayers? I tended to go with the idea it was just my breath and prayers working and that the crystal was just a comfort tool. My grandmother always told me to just take a little of everything you learn, take a pinch of the knowledge and put it in your toolbox to use at an appropriate time. I always did this except one time and that was when I became a Baha'i.

Sparrow Hawk was really getting to me with his protective shield when he showed me the finished product. It was like a shield made out of solid copper long enough to cover him from his heart area down to his knees, and he had all kinds of crystals embedded in it. He kept saying that it would reflect to where you wanted it to go. I was getting messages from spirit at this time that I needed to start sharing openly what I have learned with other people because they needed to know this. At so many gatherings, we were always told not to write anything down and not to share it with Europeans. I can understand how all these things came about in many ways from the past experiences of most Native cultures, after all their ceremonial practices became legally outlawed.

The message also said that we have to start sending the energies that we work on to the other side of Mars. All this made sense to me; the earth has taken enough and needs a break from all the negative energy have put onto it.

With all this in mind, I finally said to Sparrow Hawk, "OK, I will let you help me just this once and that is it, period, no more." I think it was more to keep him quiet than anything else.

We went over and over what we were going to do. We would do it in the ocean just off Dallas Road in Victoria. In my prayers it came to me that the entity would not go into the salt water. So off to Victoria we went to work on the client, who I had met at an earlier date, to talk about her problem, and sure enough it was located in the solar plexus area. We met her near the duck pond on Dallas road and walked to a quiet place in a secluded little cove down on the ocean. So here we all were standing in the ocean, Sparrow Hawk standing in front of her with his copper shield protecting himself, and me behind her so I could be ready to push the entity out of her. Before I did these things, I scanned the client and went over her to see what I felt along with speaking to the entity inside, telling it what I'm doing.

I started by doing my prayers first; once this was done, I started my breathing and conversing with the entity and the person, so that everyone knew what was going on, especially my spirit guides. I felt when it was ready to go and relieve its host of the overwhelming power it had over her. When I pushed out, there was a huge bang, and Sparrow Hawk fell backward into the water. He looked as if he needed toilet paper majorly; I didn't know what was on his mind, but I didn't think he had any idea what was about to happen, even though I had told him that was what would happen. He started looking in the water right away for some of his crystals that were knocked off his shield by the impact. The woman said that she felt better right away, which from my own experience I knew to be a fact. As soon as the spirits leave you, your whole body feels at ease automatically. I truly believe that we sent it to the other side of Mars where we directed it.

Sparrow Hawk went quiet after this experience; he hardly ever talked about it again. I wish I could have seen the expression on his face, along with the fear that came from deep inside him that cut the air like the sound barrier being broken. I can't for the life of me understand why anyone would want to do this kind of work; it is beyond my imagination as to why anyone would wish this upon himself.

I went back up to my home on the mountain to continue my healing path. I still had quite a long way to go, as I was only at my stomach chakra. Before you knew it I was getting red, then all of a sudden orange would start coming into my vision with my eyes closed tight. From what I was gathering, you had to have all your chakras wide open, and then you would be allowed to leave your body. When I got to my solar plexus area, where we are taught our soul sits, the color was yellow, so I used the image of an onion, peeling all the layers out of my plexus and opening the lilies around the seat of my soul. Now when I went into my meditation I would get the three colors: red, orange, and yellow. It seemed to me once I started getting these colors, it meant I had cleaned the chakra out and could move on to the next one. I will never forget the experience when my heart opened up, there were colors of greens and magenta going off like an electrical storm. It seemed to me that my heart was rejoicing beyond this earthly plane, saying, "Thank you, thank you for paying attention to me!" Then it was onto the throat chakra. It was a medium-dark blue. Funny how it seemed I was getting a sore throat as I worked on it, but I did the breath and cleaned it out with the visualization of sandpaper and the flowers started opening their petals up in a major way. The fun started when I hit the third eye area that was kind of a maroon color. I would have been afraid if I wasn't in my protection area, as there were a lot of spirits coming to me and telling me what I needed to do as I was getting closer to my crown chakra. They were telling me that I needed to visualize a sixty-four-sided crystal after I cleaned all my chakras out, and that it would spin above my head between the eighth and ninth chakra. It would be spinning and when it stopped, that facet would open up, and I would leave my body. I started getting the idea that it was like a drag race as an analogy. I would start at the bottom and the light would go to the top and when they are all lined up, I would leave my body. I knew I had to have no fear but couldn't help but wonder, how do you come back?

After eight months of working on my chakras, I was getting close. My whole being could feel this, the anticipation of leaving my body was becoming the only thing I could think of. It seemed a tease when I got to my crown and the faceted crystal would spin in front of me, just spinning as if to say you have to be totally clean first before I will even slow down. The crown chakra at the top is only one lily to open up, but there was a lot of work in this area to wrap your head around. After all, that is where a lot of our problems exist, in our minds, so in a way we are our own worst enemies. It became all about the white light. It seemed like the last potion in the mix before it would work was to get that white light shining through the colors of the heart and soul. When the day came, I wasn't really ready for it. The colors just went click, click, click, then the white light came. As it shone brightly, the multifaceted crystal stopped and invited me in. I left my body. Thank goodness I was in my star tetrahedron of protection. It gave me the feeling that I was impermeable in all ways. This happened so fast that I couldn't think of anything but getting back, which I did with no problem. All I did was think it and there I was back in my body. I started not talking about things as much, and I could tell right away what people were thinking; I could read them like a book, which I did. I couldn't wait to try it again.

My wife at the time was riding her bike up and down the rough mountain road. She was losing weight like crazy and the muscles were popping out of her legs like crazy, too. I knew she was having a very hard time, but she would never talk about it. Her mom was going through Alzheimer's; she was very concerned about this because she had told her family that she would take care of her mom. She also was very worried that she would get this dreaded disease herself. When I first met her mom, she came to the door in her bra and panties, looked around as if we weren't there, and proceeded to walk out onto the street. My wife's dad was beside himself trying to take care of her. He was getting no sleep at all and was really getting run down. The family had a meeting at this point and found a place for her to stay on Salt Spring, and it was great to have her close. It made it a lot easier on Kimi.

I did my prayers and asked for only good spirits to come to me, I put myself in the white ball of light and got into my star tetrahedron. I did some more prayers and started breathing from my bottom chakra and worked my way going up. The colors came like lighting up a Christmas tree and when I got to the top crown chakra the crystal came and stopped allowing me to leave. I left my body and went up onto what they call "the grid," there I met a lot of astral travelers including my Atlantan friend, Electron, who watched over me. I wanted to go back, whether I liked it or not, I knew I had some fear in me. When I went back into my body, my wife was there and was very perplexed. How could she not be? There was the apparently lifeless body of her husband in front of her when she walked into our home. She was not happy at all. I thought I was beside myself at this point, but this was something right out of the universe of illusion, beyond the normal curriculum we all experience. After things settled down, I said I wouldn't do it any more and I didn't, because I think deep down after all this time I was afraid of what I was doing. I would just stick with my breath for healing and stay in this realm.

After studying the law books in Victoria, I started to realize that we were going to lose the court case. The first lawyer who wrote up our agreement had made a huge and fatal mistake, which was very evident to everyone after reading the Partition Act. The group that was formed to save the Mill Farm was doing everything they could do to raise money at this time. If I had any money and enough time I would go over on the ferry to the mainland and go out to Chilliwack and take part in some circles that happened out there. They asked me to come, especially when they were planning the next medicine wheel.

It was really hard for me to travel because I had no money. They talked about the upcoming wheel and what was going on with their healing lodge society. I really never paid much attention to the Grand Mother's healing lodge; I was far more interested in the medicine wheel talk. I was saving money to be able to license my old pickup truck and go mushroom picking after the medicine wheel. Some of the young guys from Salt Spring wanted me to go and talk to the local chief in a good manner and ask him if we could go over onto his territory to pick pine mushrooms. I was planning this along with a few of the young guys on the island. I stayed pretty close to the mountain doing my prayers and just hanging out, gardening and building that fridge I told you about. As I sit here writing this, it is fifty below outside, and I wonder what I am doing to myself. Well, the deal is I have to write about this and share my story. They say everyone has a story in them, and it is good to sit down and write about your life and look in the mirror as you do so. For me it has always been the best therapy around. It is your mirror to look into, not someone else's, it is yours alone. Point a finger at someone, and you are really pointing three right back at yourself.

SUN DANCE INTRODUCTION

The medicine wheel was coming up, and I was really excited about going. This would be the third year of this wheel, I realized, because when we walked into that clearing last year that was the second year of the Elders Medicine Wheel.

I built a camper on the back of my old pickup truck to make it feel like home. There was talk about what the Grand Mother did with her society out in Chilliwack. She had started a program where she would go inside prisons and have circles with the inmates. That is how she would get a lot of the work done at the wheels; the inmates would get day passes through the Grand Mother's society. They would be released for the day by getting approval on an escorted time-away pass, commonly called an ETA. She started telling me a lot about this program that she was doing. The guys would come out and talk to the kids in school in circles. It was a great program to reconnect offenders with the community. It gave them time to get to know the people around them before they were released into the communities.

I met a guy who came to Salt Spring from the mainland to run a sweat lodge; my friends invited him to meet me. The bucket man, who was running the lodge, invited me to a Buffalo Sun Dance down in the States. I always wanted to go see a Sun Dance, which I have heard about many times and was on display in a Museum in Banff, Alberta. The display was of a Sun Dancer being hooked to the tree of life. It seemed to happen all at once. I got invited to go to a Sun Dance in Merritt from a lady who lived on Salt Spring. I found out the details, one of which said no pork or dogs were allowed on the grounds. Oh yeah, also chickens weren't allowed because it was the Eagle Sun Dance.

I really wanted to go, so when the date come up, off I went to Merritt after stopping off in Chilliwack for a night of storytelling from the old Grand Mother who would put me up in her extra bedroom. She really had a lot of great stories from the early years. Her dad was a healer and would run a sweat lodge on their territorial land near Kamloops, BC. As a little girl she would have to go get wood and water for the ceremony. What I liked about her story was that her dad did the same things that I was taught. He received a tobacco offering, and the people would say what they needed healed, then he would build a sweat lodge especially for that ceremony. When it was over, he would burn the lodge. In the stories she told me, I learned a lot of important teachings that were very similar to the prairie teachings that I had already learned. The lodges are so specific like this because spirit witnesses the tobacco being passed, which means spirit is going to be with you to help you during the ceremony. This is what a lot of people have a hard time understanding. When you say I can do that, all I need is one hundred dollars to do it, I'm taught that the spirit will not be there. As a result I have never charged money for doing a ceremony to this day, as it weighed very heavily on me, in many different ways. Once the healing sweat is over, the main reason we burn it is to pray for all the spirits that have come. By burning the lodge and prayer flags, we make sure that they don't get held up in the willows of the lodge. It is also very important to burn the cedar boughs on the floor of the lodge. By doing this you have completed your prayer circle and have finished your healing ceremony.

I got a ride from an elder on the board of the Medicine Wheel Society who was doing language workshops in Merritt. It was great getting a ride with her and chatting. As I write about this, it is wonderful how my mind still remembers that a spirit came in her car when we entered the Cold Creek area. We both recognized it at the same time. I said how honored we were that it was visiting us and asked her to pull over so that we could offer tobacco. She was very happy to have felt the energy of the spirit and asked me if I would set up a lodge on her reserve that was near Hope.

CLEANSING CEREMONY

I had come to know her house and where she lived very well. When I was staying with the Grand Mother, she said, "Oh, I'm so glad you are here. I need to do a cleansing ceremony and need your help." She filled me in about how she did the ceremony. She told me about how spirits can be so hard to help sometimes; she said the worst one she could remember was on a reservation east of Hope. There was a man who was very distraught over something and took his own life in his house. A family member moved in to make it his home, children and all. The cupboard doors started opening up right away, freaking the children out because they didn't understand what was happening. The parents understood that it must be the spirit of the person who took his life in that very house. So they got some medicine people in to do a ceremony, which they did. The spirit never went away, so the family moved out of the house. A house that's in good shape doesn't sit empty very long, and another family moved in. The same thing happened. They felt they were ready for the spirit, but one night as they were sitting there and watching TV, the spirit floated right by them as they sat on their couch. They moved out the next day. This was after the third attempt to remove the spirit. As the old Grand Mother told me the story, she said if they would have asked me, the Creator would have helped the confused spirit to the other side, and they wouldn't have had to burn the house down. Yes, you heard me right; they gave up and burned the house down. She was trying to instill the fact into me that it is always possible to help a spirit beyond this world that we live in.

This would be the third time that she had gone to the house of this elder who gave me a ride to Merritt. She had lost her husband of many years just the year before and was having huge problems with the cupboard doors opening themselves. They had done two cleansing ceremonies already, and the second time they burned everything that was his. They really believed his spirit was returning for something that was still in the house, which held his spirit back from going to the other side. After they did the second ceremony, the very next night the cupboard doors kept opening, and they started to realize it was always the same cupboard door under the sink. So then they went back to cleanse the house again for the third cleansing of the home.

What you do is plan out what you are going to do and the songs that are going to be sung. A person like me goes first with the eagle fan and a smudge bowl with sage burning in it. You go through the house in a clockwise manner, each person smudging, then the Grand Mother saying her prayers and explaining to the spirit what we were doing and that we were here to help them on their journey. People play the drums and sing near the back of the place. The route is figured out first, and at the end of the planned passage through all rooms, cupboards, closets, shelves, everywhere there is a nook and cranny, you smudge it and pray. You even go through every dresser drawer, everything, and as you keep praying, you are pushing the spirit ahead of you. Then you come to a window that is always opened a bit on the north side of the house.

When you get to this point there are special prayers and songs that are sung to help the spirit journey to the other side. When you feel the spirit is gone, you smudge the whole house again with sweet grass to bring the goodness back.

So what happened during this third cleansing was that it started in the kitchen. The excitement vibrated in my heart with every drumbeat as every cupboard door was opened. Then the doors were opened under the sink as it was being smudged, and someone noticed a built-in compartment at the back of the pipes hanging down from the sink. When they discovered it and opened it, what did they find but a full bottle of whiskey. This is why that door would open around 5:00 p.m. every day; that is the same time the husband would have a swig of whiskey when he was alive. So right away the bottle was emptied into the sink and taken to the fire outside and thrown in. This is why you talk to the spirit as if it is right in front of you, which it is, in order to explain everything you are doing. In this case talking to the spirit when you know what was holding them up on this side so they can feel free to go home to their past generation on the other side. The ceremony continued on through the house with the spirit in front of the group and when the time came at the end of the route through the house the spirit was allowed to leave through the open window. From that day forward, the woman never had a sleepless night again. Her husband was finally resting in peace on the other side.

MERRITT SUN DANCE

I had no idea whatsoever what I was getting into by showing up at this Sun Dance in Merritt. It was early, I had gone two days early so I could help setup. I was asked right away who I was and told some of the rules about how pork and chicken were outlawed on the grounds, along with booze and drugs. I always think of this man I was asked to help who had a brand-new truck. It seemed to make no difference when we were throwing shade material on his truck. He didn't care whatsoever that his new truck was getting scratches all over it. All he said was that it was just another tool for us to use. We were getting shade while another crew was getting the poles erected for the arbor and walkway that went around the outside, creating a circle with a big opening to the east where spirit came in at the other directions there was small openings, making doorways. The arbor was at the west end; this was a square area at the end of the circle, and it made a huge shade area for the dancers to go and rest under out of the sun after their rounds of dance. Once the poles were in place we would load up shade that was from the poplar tree branches. All day we did this going to get shade and spread it over the arbor and the walkway.

We did this until the head of the Sun Dance said, "That's enough, boys. Let's eat." They sure fed everyone very well; it felt like a huge family coming together for a meal. After the meal we were told to start getting willows for the sweat lodges, so off we went down the river to find the willows. Before cutting them down the man with the truck did prayers for the willows that were about to give their lives for the sacred sweat lodges. On one side of the arbor at the back there were going to be four sweat lodges built on each side of the sacred fire, four lodges for the women and four for the men. When we returned with the willows, I was surprised that they asked me to say some prayers before some of the willows were put into holes that were premade with a wooden stake.

At the Sun Dance, they only used eight willows; the lodges were small and hot with only seven grandfathers used. The grandfather pit dug in the middle of the lodge was small and deep. Once all the framework of willows was put up, a truck pulled up with large canvas tarps, which were thrown over the willow frames of the lodge, covering it all with only one dark canvas tarp. They did the same thing we would do and sent someone inside to see if there was any light coming in.

The head of the Sun Dance finally said, "Well, boys, that's a good day you have all put in. Spirit thanks you for this and wishes you a good night's sleep."

I had my little dome tent, which I set up on the edge of the people's campsite—basically anywhere outside the arbor and the cooking tent area. When I was setting up, the main fire keeper told me to tie this red ribbon on the door of my tent. He said you will need it to keep the Hyoka out of your camp. I said great I would pray and do that. After I hung it up, I sure kept my ears open trying to learn about the Hyoka, which I knew was a very strong medicine person who did everything backward.

The fire keeper said at the end of the next day there would be a tepee where the blanket men sit and take pledges, and he said it is a real learning experience to be a fire keeper. As a guest of this territory who was just learning about the Sun Dance, I never talked too much about myself; I just wanted to respect their ways and learn as much as I could in hopes that one day I could become a Sun Dancer. I slept like a log that night; I felt like I really put a hard day's work in. I heard the wake-up call. There was always the same blanket man who would arise early before sunrise and beat his drum and walk around camp.

Every once in a while he would say, "OK, all you helpers, time to rise and shine." Breakfast was always the first order of the day for helpers, and it was a great feeling that the helpers got served right after the old ones were served. Today there was some major things that needed to be done, all the tepees needed to be set up (there were eight of them). As the lodges were set up, four were on each side, as were the tepees—four for the men dancers and four for the women dancers. Yes, you heard me right, women dancers. I got on tepee setting-up duty; I told them that I had some prior experience with setting them up. When the man we worked with set the three main poles up, I was surprised how it was very similar to the way I set up tepees. The Sun Dance colors were tied in each direction as the four different directions were set up. After the poles were set up, the canvas tepee covers were tied to the smokestack pole and up the tepees would go. He was good, all the frames that we set up were good, only one gave us trouble with the length and he dug the poles into the earth that were sitting too high. There were always little tricks to every trade. Then we had to dig the tree of life hole, which was dug at least six feet deep. First, tobacco and prayers were offered, then a red cloth was put over the hole.

After supper we had one more major chore to do, and that was the sacred fire pit, which was at the farthest end of the circle on the inside. They prayed and marked it out in the shape of a buffalo footprint. It was huge, about ten feet across and eight feet wide. It was dug around sixteen inches deep into the ground at one end and even with the ground on the other end, which made it look like a buffalo footprint. Once this ceremonial fire was lit, the next day it would keep burning for the four-day period of the dance and would be kept going until the blanket men thought that all the supporters were at home. It usually went low one day and then was stoked up the last night and finally left to go out on its own.

After a few little touch-ups, we were ready for the first day of dancing. A lot of dancers were showing up during that day. Some of them were very chatty and then there were others that seemed to be in their own world lost in their thoughts. There were so much things they had to be gotten ready, like their headgear, wristbands, angle bands, and their sacred sage wand that they danced with. During that day I got lucky and was asked to go and collect buffalo sage, which was off the reservation above Merritt. The best thing about this was that I learned of a new place to collect sage. We usually collected brush sage, and I had no idea that buffalo sage grew around here, but as I learned it sure enough does. The sage was very important for the making of their regalia because it has a lot of length and is easier to tie into the headgear band that they were making.

There was a little tepee set up at the edge of the circle on the outside. This is where White Buffalo Café woman was staying. She was fasting for four days and nights before the dance, praying for all the dancers and helpers who were on their way here and for the Sun Dance itself.

Everyone was called to go and get the tree of life, which was chosen a few days before by one of the red-blanket men. It was a popular tree that was referred to as the tree of life. It was an amazing ceremony with many prayers and spiritual drumming songs. The reader has to understand that every song that is sung is a prayer song to send your prayers to the Creator of us all.

There were the little tree choppers all dressed up in cute dresses and ribbons. The girls were young in age—before they even had had their first moon. Speaking of moons, it is the same as the medicine wheel there is an area set aside so that all the woman on their moon can go into the moon lodge with the grandmothers. There seems to be always a woman who needs to be talked into going into the moon lodge and told that they aren't allowed in the circle because of the power they have while being on their moon. One woman was so upset she left the grounds and stayed in Merritt.

After the prayers were said to the sacred tree, the little tree choppers would take their little axes and chop in a different direction, each of the four tree choppers would chop the tree in one direction. Once this was done, a lot of the dancers would tie their ropes up high on the tree. They didn't want the tree to just crash down onto the ground; it was to be held back and lowered softly to the ground. At this time all the women put their shawls on the ground so that every leaf would be caught as the tree came down. Then the dancers got a bigger ax and took turns felling the tree. Just as it was ready to fall everyone held onto the ropes, to let the tree down gently. Once it was lying on the ground on top of the shawls the blanket man got all the dancers and male supporters to get under the tree and carry it to the Sun Dance grounds. Once it was in the air the tree could not be let down. The women came behind picking up their shawls, some of which had some leaves in them. The tree of life was about twelve inches at the bottom, so it is a good-size tree. We had to carry it up a hill to the grounds. Along the way we would take a break by standing still and still holding the tree on our shoulders. The drummers would sing songs as we carried the tree of life. When a dip in the ground came up, you would lose the weight upon your shoulders and then all of a sudden you would gain a lot of weight back. After a few breaks, we made it to the circle that we had to walk around to the eastern doorway, to enter the sacred circle. Just before we reached the hole, all the shawls were laid upon the ground and small logs standing upright, so that the tree could sit upon them and not be lying on the ground. There were a lot of prayers being said, lots of drumming and a pipe ceremony. After the pipe ceremony, the blanket men went to the hole where the tree was going to be planted and made offerings to Mother Earth and placed some items wrapped up in red material. While all this was going on, the tree was cleared of branches and any short ends. The first seven feet of the tree were slathered in buffalo fat and pipe stone dust, which, when mixed with the fat, turned a beautiful earthy red color. All cuts and scratches on the tree had this bloodred fat rubbed into them. Some of the branches were tied together and tied onto the tree about three-fourths of the way up. Once the branches were tied into place, they tied a cutout buffalo on one-side and eagle feathers on the other end. The eagle faced east and the buffalo faced west, both were tied up high in the tree on the outstretched arms of the branches that were tied together. Then all the dancers tied there ropes high up in the tree below the cross arms of the branches. Each dancer after they tied the ropes to the tree they would take their ropes in the opposite direction the tree was laying. After a few prayers and final explanations the red-blanket man said, "Hooka," which meant to pull and lift, so that all of a sudden the helpers were lifting the tree from the top and moving along it with a rope still trying to lift it as it went into the air. With all the dancers pulling on their ropes, the tree went up real easy and at the right angle dropped six feet to sit on the bottom of the hole. We slowly filled it and packed the new space with dirt in the hole, so that it would be tamped tight to hold the giant tree upward. It was an amazing site while all this was going on, with everyone in camp in the middle of the circle. As soon as it got into the air the Sun Dancers spaced themselves evenly all around the tree to make sure that it stood erect and straight up and down as we tamped the earth. One of the men stood away back and would make sure with a few little finger gestures that we were able to get the tree straight up and down.

Once it was up, all the branches were tied around the base of the tree, with all the leaves on the ground at the tree's base. The tree of life was ready for the ceremony to begin the next morning.

All the dancers had already done their vision quests; one of the pledges that people take is to do a vision quest before they dance. The Sun Dancer needs to do the vision quest for four days and three nights without food and water every year while being a dancer. The grounds were abuzz with all kinds of activity, as a lot of families were in their camps helping their family members get ready for this evening ceremony, where there was going to be a feast at suppertime. A lot of people referred to it as the "last supper," where all the dancers ate their last dinner before going into their tepees and awaiting the morning sunrise ceremony. Right after supper, people would say, "See you later," because it was the last time that they could talk to their family member for several days. Already I was being asked to do things from some of the dancers, like bringing hot coals into their tepee so that they could do a smudge before they bedded down. I was keeping my eyes open to see when the blanket men would be taking pledges for what you wanted to do during the dance. I saw some action happening in one corner of the arbor, which looked like what I was looking for; it was a line-up outside of the blanket men's tepee. I got into the line-up of laughing bodies of men and women. It seemed to take forever that I had to wait in the line-up. The blanket men asked who I was and asked why I had come to the Sun Dance, I told them that my heart brought me here with the intent to support the dancers and that I would like to be the fire keeper. They said that was the most sought-after position, being fire keeper, and they were pretty full because a lot of guys kept coming back to be fire keepers, but since I had some experience they let me be a fire keeper. They gave me a ribbon, which signified by its color that I was a fire keeper. I was told who to go to and tell them that I was a fire keeper and they would give me a time to do my shift. I wasn't surprised that I was given the night shift to watch the fire. I didn't realize at the time how this shift would work out to my benefit. As a side note, I had brought the two feathers that I had earned in Alaska, one from the old man and a white one from the talking stick.

The first day was a big ceremony because the sacred fire had to be lit. It was similar to starting a sweat lodge fire; many prayers would need to be said before it was lit. It also had to be lit up before the sun rose. After the fire was lit and the grandfathers put in, we all went for breakfast as the dancers hung out under the arbor. Once the grandfathers were hot enough all the dancers lined up to have their sweats. Every day the dancers would have a sweat in the morning before they started dancing, then also at nighttime, right after doing their twelve rounds of dancing they would have a sweat before going to bed.

The next morning was the first round of dancing as the sun came up. The day started early for Sun Dancers, who had to have a sweat before sunrise and be out on the grounds all sweated up and ready to dance the first dance of the day as the sun came up over the hill. The male dancers would go into the western entrance to do the first dance and welcome the sun after doing songs to the Creator. The dancers kept tune to the drumbeat as they had their hands in the air, with an eagle fan in the heart-side arm and a sage wand in the other. The women would dance in the outside walkway just outside the main circle, protecting the male dancers. The men wore headbands made out of buffalo sage; the two ends would cross in the middle of the head, coming out beyond the forehead about eight inches, which would create good protection from the sun getting into the eyes. They also wore anklets and wrist bracelets made out of sage tied together with red material. The men wore only red, knee-length skirts. Each round there were four songs sang, one in each direction. During the day there was twelve rounds; remember that dancers don't eat or drink any liquids at all for four days and nights.

After my night shift at the fire, I would go out to welcome the dancers in the morning for the first round before sunrise. I was told it was really good for the dancers to see supporters on the sidelines as they were dancing. The support meant a lot to the dancers who were sacrificing themselves for the people. I really felt the urge to be a Sun Dancer. I loved feeling the feeling of spirit being present here on these sacred grounds that sat high above the Cold Water River, meandering by in pools and eddies of melted glacier waters. When I stood on the sidelines, I held the feather that the old man gave me from Alaska. I really wanted his energy here with me. During the four days I stood on the sidelines of every dance, I would stand and move my feet to the beat of the drum. One of the main fire keepers told me one day near the end of the dance is that I should come to a pledge meeting and pledge to be a dancer. They had a pledge meeting at the local community hall, once a month during the winter.

So now I really wanted to be a Sun Dancer and had been asked by two different societies to be one. This really kept me busy and helped me a lot to forget about my everyday life of worrying myself sick about the Mill Farm Cooperative situation, which wasn't getting any better. When I got home all I could do was pray and meditate on the question of which dance do I pledge my support for, the buffalo or eagle? One thing that made sense to me was that the eagle was in the beginning of the doorways in the east, and the buffalo was in the northern door in the last doorway before going to the other side.

I started asking where my friend Milton was, and my prayers were answering that I should go and ask his counsel about which

Sun Dance to attend, as he was a Sun Dancer himself. I started learning where he was and that he had gotten married and had a place over on Vancouver Island, near Coombs somewhere.

I finally found out where he lived, and on one of my wife's days off, we went to find my old friend. When we got to the area where I heard he lived, I asked at the local grocery store where he currently lived and they told me I was very close, that it was just down the road. It sure is good how spirit works. When we pulled up I could see smoke rising in the backyard. When we went into the house it was abuzz with people cooking and getting ready for a feast. I had perfect timing and was told that they are in the middle of the second round. They said, "Here is a pair of shorts. You had better get changed and get yourself in there."

As I stood there waiting for the second round to end, I heard the familiar old call, "All my relations," and the young fire keeper opened up the door to a blast of thick steam. At the end of a round, the bucket man poured the rest of the water onto the grandfathers, creating a lot of searing heat via the steam created from the water hitting the red-hot rocks. When the door opened and my old friend crawled out on his hands and knees, he didn't seem to be surprised to see me after all this time. He hugged me and told me he loved me and that they were expecting me. We chatted for a few minutes while people caught their breath and gave thanks to the fire. I met everyone there that I didn't know. There were a couple of people who were sweating that I knew from the past. Off to the side, my old friend and I caught up with each other, and I told him I came for his counsel on the fact that I was invited to two Sun Dances, one being the buffalo and the other being the eagle. When I told him this, he looked at me with his usual look when I used to ask him questions like this. With his eyes he was saying, *Why ask me? You know what to do: just pray and the answer will come to you.* It sure felt good sitting in his lodge again. This was a good door for me to pray in. He asked me to sit in the west, which is for going deep inside and feeling your emotions. For the next two rounds when it became my turn to pray, I asked the creator and all the spirits for help in deciding which Sun Dance I should go to. After the fourth doorway, he said there would be a fifth round, a warriors' round. This was a very good round that was very hot and made me feel so good to be alive. I prayed for guidance trying to figure out which dance to go to. After the door opened, I felt like a new man again.

We had a beautiful feast with everyone and headed for the ferry, just barely catching the last boat. When my wife and I got home near sunset that evening, I sat praying and looking over Sansum Narrows when a big bald eagle landed in a tree right in front of our house and sat looking at us. It sat there all evening and into the night, and in the morning the eagle was still sitting in the tree facing east. In my teachings the eagle sits in the eastern door and represents vision. If this wasn't a message through divine intervention, I don't know what is. Needless to say I was stoked majorly. I got my answer: it was the eagle Sun Dance I would go to, and it's close, right in Merritt. I talked to some of the guys that I had met in Merritt and told them about my vision and that I wanted to get a ride with them when they went to the pledge meeting. They assured me that it wouldn't be until after Christmas. I was sure excited, about Sun Dancing but in reality I was sure that I would be dragged through the cooperative quagmire, but I had made my mind up 100 percent that there was no way I would sign the rezoning papers. Everything was put on hold around the house on the Mill Farm; there was no way I had any energy at all for doing things around the place. I really think they thought I would change my mind, at this point all I had gotten was threats, no summons as of yet. I would be spending a lot of time over in Chilliwack, going to circles and helping the Grand Mother out in any way I could. The next medicine wheel couldn't come fast enough for me.

PLEDGE MEETING

Before I knew it, I got a message saying that there was going to be a pledge meeting for the Sun Dance, and my brothers told me where to meet them in Vancouver so that we would all travel together in one car. Off we went to the community hall near Merritt, BC, to attend a pledge meeting. There were a lot of people there that I had met that summer at the Sun Dance. Some of the women were busy making food off in the corner. In front were four big cans that had sticks embedded in them, and the colors were on each stick. There also was the biggest star blanket I have ever seen hanging on the wall at the front of the hall. There was a huge buffalo hide on the floor; everyone would take their shoes off when they walked on the buffalo rug. There was a pipe rack with a lot of pipes lying on them, and also a big drum set up at the front. The red-blanket man taking the pledges got everyone's attention and said a prayer. The drummers sang a pipe-loading song, and all the pipes were being loaded as they sang. Then the pipes were lit and passed around so that everyone could share each pipe that was loaded. Remember, every pinch of tobacco put in those pipes has prayers in it, lots of prayers.

So when you get the pipe, you also pray and the smoke takes your prayers to the Creator along with the prayers of the pipe carriers. Once all the pipes were out, the red-blanket man sat on the buffalo robe. There was a line-up of people already waiting for their turn. When a person would go up barefooted and stand on the Buffalo robe, you would hold the pipe and hold it up in each direction and pray to the Creator. You would hold it up toward the crowd of people, as they were your witnesses. You would say your name and why you came here and what your pledge was. As I held the pipe, I told the Creator that I wanted to dance, and that this year I was dancing for the old people and the old man specifically, my old friend in Alaska. I said I would be clean of drugs and alcohol. You are telling the Creator and your community what you are going to dance for this year. It felt so good to be doing this; you sit back and listen to everyone's pledges, some for cooks, fire keepers, groundskeepers, dancer's helpers. All the help that is needed is pledged before the Sun Dance at these pledge meetings.

After everyone was done, we ate and ran, because it was a long drive back to Vancouver. Looks like I was going to have a good summer. I just went back to my old ways of getting some work whenever I could. I really never was the type of guy to hold down any kind of job for any length of time. This was a much different type of lifestyle compared to my wife who worked in the health field, with a pension and all that stuff. When I met my wife she couldn't believe that I never had medical coverage, she said when we were married I would go onto her medical, which happened. I always felt I was working in my own way, working for spirit meant I followed my dreams though not many people, including myself, could really understand this. Even to this day people ask me what I do, and forever I have been lost for words but have come to this conclusion after all these years. I say I work for spirit, and while saying it I have a huge smile of happiness and understanding on my lips that speak of peace and love. All I knew was that I was getting so excited about my coming Summer going first to the medicine wheel, then the Sun Dance and then to go picking pine mushrooms with the young men from Salt Spring.

VISION QUEST

Now was the time to get ready for the vision quest in the mountains, which in turn gets you ready for the Sun Dance. We were getting together, packing everything up and heading up to the Merritt area to sit on the mountain for four days and nights without food or water. When we got to the fasting grounds, which were close to where we went to the Sun Dance, there was no one there, so we went into Merritt to find the red-blanket man. He was the helper of the main Sun Dance man from the States that every Sun Dancer looked up to, a man I have heard a lot about but have never met.

One of the reasons you never hear me mention the names of the people there is it is out of respect for their spirits, unless it is in a ceremony like the sweat lodge. We are taught to let them go to do their work on the other side, and if we speak their names it means that we are disturbing them on their journey and holding their spirits back from doing what they are supposed to do, performing their journey on the other side. The red-blanket man who we were meeting in Merritt is the man who came to our dance to do the piercing and skin offerings. While at his place he gave us orders as to what we needed to do. My two buddies went back to the area that was picked out for the vision quest. We had a lot of work to do: getting all the willows ready for the sweat lodge, along with a lot of firewood for the sweats and the campfire, plus we had to find the grandfather stones for the lodge. I always enjoyed doing this. We would travel back into the mountains where the grandfathers had been waiting for thousands of years to give us their red-hot energy in our sweat. You would find a lava rock lying here and there. The edges would be smoothed out into round forms from being moved across the earth by the glaciers ten thousand years before, when this area was covered in a huge slab of solid ice.

We happily went about our business of getting all the materials that were asked of us before we set up our own tents. I would only be using mine for one night. The next morning more help arrived and we set up everything, the good part about all this was that I could get all my stuff ready while the helpers set things up.

I had to finish my prayer ties off for my protection circle. It being the first time that I was being put up onto the hill, I had to tie 606 prayer ties. Which meant cutting 606 pieces of material, 101 of each color in every direction and another set for the one below and the ones above. This is done so that you are covering everything and everyone possible in your prayers and not leaving anything out from your protection prayers that form a circle around you up on the hill. I never learned this the first year but I will share it with you now...actually, no, I had better wait and tell you about it when I talk about the next year. We were going to a sweat lodge first then our last supper before going up the hill for four days and nights without food or water.

Before the sweat ceremony we were told to put our pipes on the prayer mound. We would load them all together, while the pipe-loading song was being sang. Then we would put them on the pipe rack, which is made out of some willow sticks with the Y at the end, the single end goes into the ground and the Y faces up and there is a cross piece that brings them together forming a pipe rack. All six of us that were going to fast put our pipes on the rack. The idea was that our pipes could be prayed for and give us strength while we were up on the hill, then we would smoke them when we came down from the hill after our vision quest and smoke them in the sweat.

After the pipes were loaded and put onto the rack, the red-blanket man walked up and asked, "Whose pipe is that?" as he pointed at mine. My stomach did a roll of fright, as it tightened into a fearful knot. I said that it was mine in a sheepish voice. He said, "I haven't seen that pipe stem in many years. Where did you get it from? It is my grandfather's and has been in our family for many years." I told him that a friend of mine, Milton, gave it to me when he came back from Sun Dancing in Manitoba a few years back. He responded, "Ah well, it is good to see my old friend again. I gave Milton that pipe stem. Now I know who you are—he talked about you at that Sun Dance. You're the young man he met and you live up on a mountain. Now your story makes sense to me as I see your pipe."

The sweat lodge was really good. He explained a lot of things that we needed to do when we got up the hill, how to put our protection out around us and make our little altar at one end of our circle on the inside of the prayer ties and now I knew why we were asked to bring a little knife: it was to split the storms that we saw coming so that they would go around us.

After having a full belly, we were all ready to head up the hill, in front would be the blanket man and the drummers and singers, along with one drummer at the back of the line. One of the hardest things was to tie your 606 prayer ties that are all tied in one line, which is really long, and not to get them tangled up. You have to keep them all in order of their colors. So basically what you have is 101 pieces of red, two-inch-by-two-inch material. When you are praying, you take a pinch of tobacco and pray for everything in that direction. By having 101 squares in each direction prayed upon and tied off in the string that you use, it forms a nice little ball as you tie it off. With so many prayers it allows you to include everyone in your prayers from the heart. As you finish your prayer, you wrap the string four times around the piece of material and tie it off with a special knot so that it won't fall off. You really don't want any falling off. You place them about two inches apart from one another. This gives you an idea how long the line is. Now I'm curious thinking about it, so I'll do that math. Two times 606 is 1,212 inches long. I feel like I'm back in school; after all, I did make it to grade six, so I think I can do this by dividing by twelve and getting 101 feet long. That is why I said it is very hard to keep these prayer ties from getting tangled up.

So up the hill we went, and as we went up the blanket man said, "OK, you go here," and pointed to a spot that was fairly level and on a cliff ledge overlooking the valley and some fields. They wait and then help you to spread out your prayer ties in a circle. When you have made four willow sticks with the main colors tied on them, you then place each one in its appropriate direction, about seven feet apart. Then you start in the east with the color red, although it's actually now yellow for the sun dance, then you start spreading them out all around, until all 606 prayer ties are forming your protection circle. Then they tell you what else you need to do and they are gone, moving onto the next dancer's spot.

I had to make my own little altar with my pipe rack, place my pipe on it along with my "Waluta," my spirit protector, made of one yard of red felt material, with a pouch of tobacco put in the middle and tied off with sinew, an abalone button, and an eagle feather. It is the most amazing-looking prayer tie when you place it in your circle; it actually looked like a spirit was looking over you. Then in front of your altar you would place the knife with the blade facing out and pray that the knife will split the storms so that they will go around you. You have a blanket with you to keep warm, and we are told to try and stay awake the whole time to be ready when spirit comes to you. We have been taught that if you are ready, they will take you away on the fourth night. When you have the entire protection circle ready, you pray and smudge the inner circle so that it is clean of all energies.

We take a braid of sweet grass with us to create a doorway when we leave our circle; the only reason you would need to leave your circle is to do your personal business, or when your body is saying you need to go. You take the sweet grass and lay it over your prayer ties so that as you step on it you also are pulling it up at the same time. This makes it so you are closing the door right behind you, so that nothing comes in your sacred space. Then you do the same procedure as you go back into your protection circle.

The first night went really well; after all, I had a full belly and my lips were still wet from my last drink of water for four days. It was so nice to be sitting there welcoming the new morning, as the light of day shone its brilliance upon the good earth. You could see the river flowing by at a distance and the mountains loomed up all around you, in all different shades of light and shadows of dawn.

I figured out later how they work out where they put you on the mountain. Early that morning, it was around May 22, when the frost was out of the ground, a farmer came to work his fields, which was a real distraction for me. Especially when, later in the day, a pickup truck drove up to the tractor in the field and stopped to have what I'm sure was lunch with the man driving the tractor. This went on every day I sat on that hill overlooking this huge piece of farmland, by the river, where it had washed all the soil down over the centuries from the mountains surrounding it. A hummingbird came right up to me as I sat cross-legged, praying in my circle, trying to get the vision of food out of my mind. The water thing wasn't too bad because of my breathing exercises. I knew where there was a creek about two miles away, and I would pray and send my energy there to spiritually drink from the stream. This really helped more than I could imagine, incredibly spirit was there helping me. I sat in the north of my circle and always prayed for the old man in Alaska to come to me, wishing he was there with me. I tried to stay awake, but I know I must have nodded off here and there throughout the night. When I awoke that morning, I was so surprised that chills ran up and down my spine. I felt my prayers were answered big-time; in the north all my prayer-tie strings had been separated like someone had cut them. They had to have been cut because there were six laps of sinew together overlapping one another at least six times, maybe even eight times. There was no pair of hands in existence that could break them apart, but spirit could, and that is why I felt my prayers were being answered by spirit. Later that day one of the guys went walking down the hill with his gear, he got what we call "scared off the hill," because he said he felt a spirit visit him in the night, and he just couldn't sit well with it and had to leave the hill. This meant there would be no dancing for him at the coming Sun Dance. Oh yeah, I forgot to tell you there were two women doing a vision quest also, but they only had to go up for two days and nights, because they were caregivers.

At nighttime you wouldn't see the blanket men, but they would come to check on you. Their way of checking on you was to sing you a song, one that gave you so much strength in your heart just by hearing it and feeling the vibration of the drum. It gave you the strength for another night. A human voice did ask, "Are you all right?" It was their way of offering you an olive branch. I just sat there praying and never said a word. Why I never said a word was because it gave me strength to feel that I was not part of this world, that I was experiencing what it was like on the other side, so I didn't speak.

The last day came, and was it ever hard. I knew whoever was delivering that lunch in the field below must have had a big jug of ice-cold water, along with the lunch that they were sharing. My lips and mouth were so dry, I don't now how I did it. I was absolutely determined not to be chased off the hill, if only I could just make it one more night. As I smacked my lips together, there was no more saliva in my mouth at all. It was a very discomforting feeling.

Well, I made it, the red-blanket man and the helpers came up the hill to get us later that morning. We were told not to say anything until we were in the sweat. I was so parched I don't know if I could have spoken anyway. As we went down the hill, we picked up a faster who had berry stains all over his lips. Everyone laughed when they saw him.

He grinned and said, "They were right in front of me. I figured I had better remove them from temptation," and then we all laughed together. Like I said, on the first vision quest they will often do that. In fact there was another guy that they put right on the riverbank. He said he never took a swallow of water even though it was right there tempting him during the entire four days. When you think about it, it is a good exercise to do it this way, because it shows you how to pray harder and remove those distractions from your being. It is all part of the four-year journey that you have pledged for.

Man, did it feel good to have a sweat and come back to life! They give you chokecherry juice, which brings you back to life and also cleans out anything that you are holding in. They give it to you before the sweat, so that you are cleaned out spiritually, physically, emotionally, and mentally before the sweat starts. During the sweat when it became my turn to speak, I talked about how hard it was to get rid of the distractions around me. That's when they told me that was why they set me up like that on the first vision quest that I had, to learn to overcome distractions. I talked about my prayer ties being cut in just the north direction, which they had all witnessed when they picked me up that morning. They said they took it as a sign that my prayers were being answered. We all smoked our pipes before the sweat began in the lodge as we sat inside before the first round. The rounds were very fast and to the point because we were all so weak.

The vision quest was one of the best things that I have ever done in my life. I was now ready to dance my first Sun Dance, which was sadly the last Sun Dance in Merritt. Now that the four-year cycle was up, I got real lucky because it meant that I would be able to go to a different Sun Dance to complete my four-year cycle.

When I came back to the mountain, all I could think about was the Sun Dance, which was coming up in July in Merritt. It was a good idea to invite a friend who would help and support you, so I invited a friend who was staying on Salt Spring at the time and who was very interested in the Sun Dance. I had to get my outfit made. It was made out of red material and went past my knees. The outfit was just a piece of material with strings on it to tie around your waist. I was so excited this year because I was going to be a dancer instead of a fire keeper.

SUN DANCE

After being home for a few months and getting ready for the Sun Dance, it was time to meet my friends in Vancouver and head to the dance. We got there early because you are supposed to be there four days before the dance in order to get ready and pray for your strength. You are there for four days of dancing, and it was taught that you should stay four days after the dance in order to absorb everything and prepare you for the outside world again. Today, not many people stay because they are always in a hurry to get back to their lives of work. I always did the twelve-day cycle. I still don't understand why people go from the dance right back into everyday life without absorbing everything what went on. People would pack up after the closing ceremony and leave. There were many stories about people getting into accidents and having problems in their lives because they left Sun Dance early. Even I witnessed this after a dance in Merritt. Some dancers left right after the dance and before they came across to the main road, their van started smoking. Then all the passengers got out to see what was going on, and the van went up in a huge ball of flames, burning everything inside. The blanket man mentioned that a spirit was telling them that they had left too early and that they should have stayed to really learn, which was no joking matter to the spirits.

We got everything together, and I took the last day to get myself ready. I had to make my headgear, bracelets, anklets, and sage wand before I could go. On the head gear, you use long main-wing eagle feathers, which was given to me by one of the brothers. When you make your headgear, it is important that it fits just right because you don't want anything falling off while you are dancing. The buffalo sage ends up being about an inch thick for your headband with the two point feathers in the middle of each side. This was wrapped and held together with a strand of red embroidery thread. Another thing that you needed was an eagle whistle that you blew to bring the eagles to the ceremony. I was lucky because Milton gave me one, which was special since he used it himself while dancing.

I was pretty sure that I was ready to go and get the sacred tree. Tree day is actually the day before you dance, and then you have your last meal and drink of water that night. I was honored to have gotten to tie my rope up onto the tree, which was around sixty feet long and made out of a hemp-like material. You must mark your own rope so that you know the rope is yours, for there are about thirty ropes tied on the tree.

As a dancer, you would tie your own rope onto the tree before the tree was raised into place. You would tie your rope in the direction that you wanted to dance. For me, it was my first year, so I danced facing east. All the dancer's ropes were tied close together and were going off in different directions. It looked like a row of ropes that were tied together at one spot, which were high up on the tree of life just below the cross branches. Once the tree was raised, all the ropes were hanging down for the dancers to grab their ropes and spread out making a circle. As the tree was set in place, all the ropes hung freely while they waited for the day you are pierced. Since it was the Eagle Sun Dance that taught compassion, we didn't pierce on the first year. In the second year, you pierce the heart side. In the third year, you pierce the other side. Finally, in the fourth year, you get pierced on both sides. Oh, wait. I am getting ahead of myself, you have no rope in your first year.

I didn't have an eagle fan, but the feather the old man gave me. After your last meal and drink, a man tells the dancers that it is time for them to go into the arbor and leave their family and friends behind. Once you go into the arbor, you can't leave until the ceremony is over. Before going, everyone talked among themselves about which tepee they all should go into. Many brothers from Vancouver and myself from the island chose to sleep in one of the tepees. Man, was that something to sleep in a tepee. If you didn't get to sleep right away, you could hear the snoring from every direction. Man, was it loud to sleep in a tepee with twelve men. The chorus of their snores would go on throughout the whole night. Before we went to sleep, we had a sweat. They were small sweats with only seven grandfathers; they don't want to take to much energy out of you. As a dancer, all you can wear is your skirt or shorts for a sweat when you are outside the tepee. So before the first sunrise ceremony, you are standing outside in the chill, waiting to get into your sweat before the dance begins.

Before the dance, you must saturate yourself with water. You often drink two gallons of water until your belly sticks out and sloshes like a balloon full of water. This is one of the secrets to being able to get through the four days without food and water.

The excitement was built in everyone to do the first dance. After the sweat, we lined up in the formation that we were expected to keep for the whole dance. The red-blanket man would smoke a pipe and pray first, then in the east we would line up in two lines because there were thirty of us. Behind the men were the women dancers who formed a circle around the outside of us for protection. The first dance and song was to honor the Creator and welcome the spirits to our dance. We would follow our lead dancer and faced the tree as we danced to the beat of the drum. When the song came to a certain point, the head dancer would turn, and we would follow his direction. We would do this for all the directions. Then after the drums stopped, the dancers would go for a rest under the arbor or into our tepees. I have no idea how long this took, but we dance like this twelve times during the day, which took from sunrise to sunset and without food or water.

We were told in the arbor that there was going to be a flesh offering, and anyone who wanted to participate could do so on the break. The dancers were offered the first chance to give their flesh. The man who did the piercings sat with a buffalo robe over his knees and asked people where they wanted to take their flesh and how much. He would take a clean surgical blade and cut a strip of the skin from wherever you wanted him to. Most people would take skin from their arms. Since it was my first year, I only wanted one strip that was four inches long taken off my heart-side arm. I had a bare-naked woman tattooed on my arm from a drunken Calgary stampede night when I was fifteen years old. I could tell that he wasn't happy with my tattoo, and I later learned that many people weren't happy about it because of the disrespect toward women. You could see him set up outside the main circle, and there was a line-up of supporters giving their flesh offerings. Once all the offerings were given, the flesh offerings were tied in a piece of buffalo leather and placed under the tree.

Another thing we had was our prayer ties for the Sun Dance. Each one is a meter of colored material. At the top of the material you would put a handful of tobacco and offer your prayers for the teachings in that direction. Then you tie it off with a piece of sinew so you end up with six different colors all tied together with the tobacco and the ends flowing down three feet.

The round came up where you offered these prayer ties to the tree along with a pouch of tobacco, which was placed on the ground. When it comes to your turn, two blanket men take you to the tree of life to offer your prayer ties. I had been warned about going to the tree and the energy that I would feel. They take your ties from you and tie them to the tree. While you place your head on the tree, the red-blanket man stands behind you and brushes you off with an eagle fan. Oh my goodness, you certainly could feel the energy. No wonder one dancer went down with the energy. It was all I could do to keep upright when the eagle fan brushed over me, especially on the area of my head. Once all the dancers were done and during the next dance, all the supporters lined up and entered the sacred circle to offer their prayer ties and tobacco.

They came through the eastern doorway. The only time anyone could come through that doorway was when the red-blanket man was doing the ceremony. Otherwise it was just the spirits who could enter through that doorway, and no one was to cross that door. No one, not even the red-blanket man. We danced the whole time. The supporters lined up and offered their prayers while they told the blanket man what to pray for as he brushed the supporters down. After all the prayers ties were offered to the tree, it looked beautiful with all the colors hanging from it. It was like a huge mass of prayers in a circle that was six feet thick. Then all the skin offerings were tied in a piece of leather and placed at the base of the tree.

That day, it was around thirty degrees Celsius. The weather was so hot that one guy just went facedown from the heat. If people were getting sunburned, they couldn't use sunblock. I got as ready as I could and took my shirt off whenever I could and walked barefoot to build up my feet. Before the dance a lot of people would walk around the circle in order to pick up rocks and sharp objects up off the ground.

It was about the seventh round of the day when we saw the sweat being fired up, which made us wonder who would want a sweat. Just after the lodge started, we saw an eagle fly low over the grounds and circle the sweat lodge just above it. What a sight that was. The eagle flew over, and out stepped the main Sun Dance leader from the States along with his brother who came up from Idaho to do the Shape Shifter Ceremony. It seemed to make sense why the eagle circled the sweat lodge low in the sky.

Five more rounds to go. We went for a break under the arbor where the uncles from the States were giving everyone a pep talk to help us through the day. They would offer the pipe in the four directions, and after that was done, we would start dancing again. On the first round of each morning, we would set our pipes on a huge pipe rack that was to carry at least thirty pipes. After we danced the twelve round, we would pick up our pipes and smoke them later in our tepees. Yeah! I made it through the first day. I went right to the tent, changed into shorts, and had a sweat. After the sweat, we would go back to our tepees to rest. Most of us were beat. We sat smoking the pipes while we prayed for strength to get through the four days. Sadly, we lost two brothers and one sister on the first day. One of the red-blanket men told us stories and wished us good-night. After a few jokes, the guys talked about food, and before you knew it, the snoring started.

It seemed that time flew right on by. You closed your eyes and the next thing you knew, you were awake from someone calling, "Hooka." It was rise and shine for the Sun Dances, which began with hitting the sweats. Before you knew it, you were putting your pipe on the rack and getting ready to dance. On the second day, some brothers would get pierced and hooked up to the tree. When the seventh round came, I saw some dancers with a round circle painted on their chests. The round circles indicated where the piercer should pierce. It took four dancers per round to be pierced because the piercings took time. During the dance, the four men's ropes were staked to the ground. Then two of the red-blanket men would come out into the circle and escort the brother to the tree and tell him to lie on a buffalo robe. They made a wooden peg out of chokecherry bush. Sharpened to a very sharp point, the peg was about a quarter-inch thick and three inches long. The piercer took a surgical knife and made two slits in the skin, then pushed the peg through the two cuts, leaving a piece of skin about a quarter-inch wide between the two slits in the flesh. The red-blanket man took the rope, which was looped with a piece of sinew and wrapped very tight on the chest-side of the peg. It had to be tied very tight because the dancers didn't want to tear their skin from their chest. Breaking free, it would just tear the one little piece of flesh out and leave a round wound in your skin on your chest.

Being so close to everyone dancing in the circle, you felt their energy. As a new dancer, I paid close attention to the dancers who were getting pierced. I noticed the red-blanket man tied the sinew around the skin and pulled it tight in order for it the skin to not rip. I also noticed that the guy's feet would point straight into the air with so much stress that you could see the veins of his feet about to burst. You could see the searing pain that went through the brother's body when the sinew was pulled tight. I knew that I needed to get an eagle fan for the next dance because we were told that when you get pierced, the eagle fan would take away the throbbing pain.

Once the brother was pierced, he stood up and pulled his rope tightly over his body and went back into the dancing formation. The rope was pulled tight as he swayed away from the tree of life. The red-blanket man stood behind him as he brushed the dancer down with an eagle fan. The dancer then danced toward the tree of life and put his head to the tree in order to pray. He did this three times with the red-blanket man who was behind the dancer and prayed for him. As they danced, they would slap their rope with an eagle fan.

When they went to the tree for the fourth time, the red-blanket man said to him, "This is your fourth time. Pray hard, my boy, pray hard to the Creator and old ones about why you are here and what you are praying for as you dance backward." As they came back into the circle, they danced backward to face the tree of life. The dancers needed to pray hard and try to break free on the first pull.

As the brothers went backward and saw the rope getting tighter, they pulled their chests tight to break free from the tree of life. Once free, there was so much tension on the rope that it flew skyward toward the tree as their skin broke free from their chested heart.

We were taught that the vision quest was to live up to our pledges of not drinking and doing drugs. Our vessel is clean, and the spirits would not let you bleed as your skin is ripped from your chest. As soon as the dancers broke free, the red-blanket man put fresh sage into the freshly broken skin, which would help heal the wound right away. During every dance, there were someone who couldn't break free and needed to be either cut free or had bled.

This told the red-blanket man that the brother needed to do some work on himself, especially if he couldn't break free. Even the dancers could feel their energy and knew that they had slipped up during the years. That was why it was so hard to dance the piercing rounds. We needed to dance the extra rounds that it took for the dancers to be pierced and to dance praying to the tree. During those rounds, we felt what was happening in the circle because we were so connected as we all danced shoulder-to-shoulder facing the tree.

I started to wonder about getting pierced. However, during the next piercing round, one of the brothers never broke loose and his skin looked like it was going to rip a huge hole out of his chest. You actually pull the tree toward you, and as the tree snaps back into place, it helps your flesh pull free from your swollen chest. This didn't help the man and whispers went down the line as we danced to pray hard for our brother. This man came to the Sun Dance but never did the vision quest before, which was one of the requirements. Yet, somehow he talked the red-blanket man into dancing. The blanket man was OK with it and left it up to spirits to dance. He got weaker and weaker as he ran to the side and just before he pulled tight, he would jump into the air to get some extra help. He did this sixteen times. He tried his hardest to break free and every time he tried we felt his energy. It was as if we were all hooked to the tree of life. After his tries, he broke down. He was like a lump of sobbing grief on the ground. Two red-blanket men came to his side and talked to him gently. When the man got to his feet, they showed him to the tree. As he held his head against the tree, the red-blanket men cut him free from the tree of life. I had no idea what this man was going through, but the whole idea of the dance was to pray and be able to break free from the tree of life, which showed that you had lived a good year and were in contact with your spirits.

After that round, the red-blanket men, along with our uncle from the States, got us all together under the tree. They gave us a little speech about how it was important to do our vision quest and to follow what we had pledged, which was held with the sacred pipe and your communities as your witness. The spirits were to look over you at all times. There was no getting away with anything while walking this life.

It was getting really hot; the sun above us burned hot and scorched people's hides, which later turned deep red. On the last day, on the sixth round, dancers were losing their steps. My friend who danced by my side was a big Cherokee man, and he, too, started to waver in the heat. His brow wilted and sagged as his eyes slightly closed. He was about to go down, but a brother on the other side helped him. Yet, just before the last song, the Cherokee man fell, and we helped him up. Sadly, that was his last round as he hobbled out of the circle. He told us that he was done, and we all felt the pain in his voice. A red-blanket man called us over and told us that we were not to interrupt the spirits' job; if a dancer was supposed to go down, let him go down. If you think about it, this was true because the main thing about Sun Dance was to experience the other side. This was my chance to feel and be with the Creator as well as the spirits on the other side. It was a good lesson for me to learn, since this was my first dance.

You might wonder if the women pierce. Yes, a few of the women pledge to pierce. They don't pierce in the first year, but in the second year, the women get their heart-side upper arm pierced. It is a smaller chokecherry peg. Two small slits are put into a woman's upper arm. Then an equal-size piece of smooth wood is put through the two slits, and an eagle feather is tied to the wooden peg. Like I said, there weren't as many women who pierced unless they had a vision to do so. However, most women did flesh offerings. The amazing thing about the flesh offerings were, they didn't even hurt much. The man who did them was an amazing gentleman. When I did it, it happened so fast that I didn't even know it was done.

Finally, the last round of the dance was sudden. Everyone was so excited that we even forgot about our dry mouths and knotted stomachs of hunger. Our thoughts were to finish the last dance round and get ready for a sweat in the lodge because you never wanted to be the last man in. The quicker the dancers could get into the sweat lodge, the sooner we would be brought back to life.

As soon as the lodges were done, all of the dancers sat facing one another in a line where the women were on one side and the men were on the other. There was a twelve-foot walkway in between and rows of tepees on each side. Before the families and support people were allowed into the inner circle, we had to be brought back to life.

They gave each dancer a glass of chokecherry juice, which was supposed to bring you back to life. It sure brought me back to life. The same time it hit my stomach, I ran to one of the outhouses.

Man, I was glad that it was empty because I needed to explode in that deep dark hole. The rumble from my stomach created a flow that I never felt, which cleaned me out in seconds. Boy, did that ever felt good. When I opened the door there was a big line-up. Some people didn't make it, but we won't talk about that.

Once everyone was done doing their business, we returned to our spots in line. We were given a glass of sweet grass tea, which brings the goodness back into your life. After this was done, people entered the tepee area to see their loved ones and friends. People gave gifts, and those who completed their fourth year received giveaways. Blankets were a big gift. It was customary to do give gifts to everyone on your fourth year, which included the red-blanket men, the cooks, fire keepers, piercers, and dancers. It was like a four-year plan to get all these gifts together. Even I started to plan my giveaways in three years.

We were given buffalo heart broth to eat, which was to ease you into the feast. We were taught to bring our own plates and utensils. The food was placed in the middle of the circle and off to one side of the tree of life. There was a huge circle as people put down their blankets and chairs to mark their spots. There were always jokes going around about sharing blankets. You needed to be careful where you sat. If you share a woman's blanket, it has a huge meaning. I will leave you to contemplate that thought.

Everyone took their spots in the circle. There was a prayer said for the food and everyone involved. Then, there was humor, and the servers started to serve the food. There were three young people to a pot. The main dish was divided up into huge pots, and I mean huge. It took two people to carry each pot and one to serve out the contents onto people's plates. After the main pots were served, the smaller platters were served. It was a huge feast, and there was food everywhere. Your plate was heaping full with meat, potatoes, rice, and vegetables. Your bowl was full of salad, and there were pieces of bannock and buns on your blanket. There were a few sad faces from those who couldn't break away. The grief was written all over their faces, and though we could see it, there was no way we could say we knew how it felt.

Back in the camp, my small quiet dome tent felt like home. After a good night's sleep, I asked my friend what the first day of dance was all about. When we were dancing, we heard hollering, and when I looked over, I saw my friend walk around the circle and past the eastern doorway where no one was supposed to walk. I eventually apologized because it was my responsibility to tell my friend to not walk by the doorway unless he was led by a red-blanket man. We had a big day ahead of us because we needed to burn everything, including the prayer ties and the tree of life. The only thing that wasn't to be burned was the main structure poles that were dug into the ground to hold the shaded branches. It took us all day. There was one brother who came back and left right after the dance, but only got two miles down the trail when his van caught on fire. Many people left early to go back to work and never did the twelve-day teaching ritual.

I was sure happy to get back over the mountain and home to my garden and family. Sadly, it was the last dance in Merritt and the word was that we would be going to Sioux Valley in Manitoba next year. However, if that was the case, we heard that there would be a pledge meeting in Vancouver. It meant that if the red-blanket men didn't set one up in BC, we would have to travel to Manitoba in order to pledge. We were told that they would let us know.

Time flew by and it was time to pack up and get ready to go to the medicine wheel. I also packed everything to go directly up to the mushroom camp. I tried saving enough money to catch the ferry and I had enough money for gas to take me up where the mushroom camp that was situated at Kitwanga, BC. It was great getting to the medicine wheel grounds a couple of days before in order for me to experience everything that went on. This huge gathering came to life with the four cedar trees and the medicine wheel of rocks in the middle. It was like being at home and welcoming everyone who came onto the grounds. The Grand Mother would show up when her tepee was set up, which was the first thing we did. At the head of the grounds and right in the middle, spots were marked out for the elders' camp. She wanted my camp next to hers, but I always liked being in the background, so I picked my camp to the side of the main camps. One of the reasons that I preferred it this way was that I was always the first one up in camp, which meant that I was the first to go to bed. It has always been my lifestyle to live in the light of day as much as I can, and I'm sticking to that story.

Once we set up the Grand Mother's tepee, the women would start putting all her stuff in the tepee. Oh my, there was so many bags of blankets and everything that it boggled my mind. Trailer after trailer of supplies from Chilliwack to the grounds were being transported. The kitchen alone was two eight-by-sixteen-foot trailers with four-foot sides that were full of materials like tarps, poles, tables, and chairs. After the kitchen was set up, another trailer would be unloaded with all the equipment to cook and serve the tasty full-course meals for the six hundred people who were expected to come. Back to the Grand Mother's tepee. The women spent most of the day getting her tepee just right, according to what she had asked her helpers to do. The ground was even covered with many different colorful carpets that made the floor vibrant in colors of the universe, which soothed your inner heart as you entered the space. The walls of the tepee were covered with all different kinds of star blankets and homemade quilts. Some nice paintings were hung on the wall along with medicines. In the middle was a fire pit, which was where we had a council meeting and had a person watch the door for us. As I write, I realize how the Grand Mother actually similar to my own grandmother; she even looked like her, with her hunched-over shoulders. The Grand Mother asked me to wake her up in the mornings. Being the first one up always meant that I had the first pot of coffee made. People were starting to arrive in great numbers the day before, to be of help setting up the camp.

Thinking of my own grandmother. When I was kid, everyone had a title except for me. We never even knew about prejudice; with all respect we called one another wops, square heads, and jungle bunnies. I would go home and ask my mom, and she said we were from here. To a young man, that meant nothing, and I wanted to tell my school counterparts who I was. All I would get was flack from my friends when they asked me. When my grandmother would stay with us, I would ask her, and she would say the same thing. That was when I gave up on my search for myself.

We did everything before the people arrived. It seemed that even the transportation of everything took at least two days of solid work. The wood alone was a massive stack. There was enough for the sacred fire to burn steadily for at least five days, including the moon lodge, and the two sweat lodges. Yes, the Grand Mother wanted wood for all the camps. Now that was a lot of wood. The guys from the local prisons with their ETA passes were great helpers in many ways. They would do anything you asked them to do with no questions at all. Everything was set up, including the sweat lodges, the moon lodge, all the tepees, and the children's area. The Grand Mother asked me to walk her around and show her everything after, which included the main inspection of the medicine wheel. As we were walking from the sweat lodge area, there walked a black bear behind us. The people watched in fear. They didn't want to shout and alarm us and the bear. We felt something but just kept walking into the clearing of the medicine wheel. The bear later turned down another path. Man, was there a lot of excitement throughout the camp as the bear walked away from us. We thought it was a great sign from the spirits.

At a council meeting there were two elderly people: a man from Keremeos and the main Grand Father of a big reserve near the University of British Columbia. It felt good to see my uncle from the States here, which was a powerful feeling happy to have the two golden eagle heads together as one. Everything was discussed at the first meeting, which was held around the Grand Mother's tepee with the fire moving and dancing to every flicker. They told me that I was to run the sacred sweat again, which made me feel good, but also sent a wave of fear through me when I heard that the council wanted me to be bucket man. Please understand that this was hard for me to write because in order to be allowed entry into the northern doorway, one must be fearless. Being in charge of the bucket meant that you knew and understood the strength of the sacred water. It was one of the most important things to understand. There had been many people burned before and who would never go back into a lodge again because of being burned by a person who didn't understand the amount of water that needed to be added to the red-hot grandfather rocks that let off a ripping, burning blast of steam.

The council decided to do the cleansing and burning ceremony on the grounds of an old residential school in the south, which had only some of the foundations left. The foundations sat like mindless monuments from the past. Some of the main parts were still used as an education center, Native art shops, and band offices. What was vacant was an Indian residential school. I was also asked to start the sacred fire this year because they knew that I didn't use paper to start my fires. Yes, I used a wooden match, though. My helpful fireman and I started the sacred fire before sunrise, which burned for at least five days. At night, there were fire keepers that made sure that the fire was kept. Being the first up to make coffee, I would take a cup of hot campfire coffee to the person who kept care of the fire over the night. He sure was always thankful for this action. My fireman attended that residential school up till the day it was shut down, which was one of the last schools to be shut down in the nineties. We got birch bark from the hillside above the grounds to start the sacred fire. He used the birch bark like newspaper and placed it on the bottom of the fire pit. This was placed on the tobacco that offered prayers to the fire pit in every direction.

Everyone got woken up by my fire keeper, who walked around the camp and played his drum. I had already woken up the elders. The sacred fire had already been prayed for and was ready to be lit before sunrise. All the people who got up early for the Morning Sunrise Ceremony were standing around the outside of the stones that made the medicine wheel. Close to the Grand Mother's tepee, there were the elders and helpers who were decked out in fancy ribbon shirts and blouses with ribbons that flowed in the breeze, ready to proceed to the inside of the medicine wheel. It was always fun to see how the Grand Mother would line up everyone. She led the lines. I became her number one and everyone would tease me for this, which I didn't mind at all. After all, it was an honor to be the one to walk along beside her with a few others she had chosen. As we walked to the medicine wheel, we would drum and sing the selected songs that the Grand Mother chose. The eagle song was always one of her favorites. When we reached the eastern doorway, there was an outline of two large grandfather rocks with each of the four doorways marked by larger stones. We would pray in each direction before we entered the inner wheel where the wood waited to be lit. The sun came over the hill at 5:30 a.m. As the sun rose over the hill, my fire keeper lit the sacred fire in each direction from the east to the north. The birch caught fire and a huge puff of black smoke went away into the air. It was funny.

Many people afterward said, "Sure, you don't use paper, but it looks like you used diesel fuel." That was why birch bark was so good to use; it had an oil-like substance in the bark that lit up easily. It was actually easier to light than paper, which could get damp.

We used birch bark many times for the sweat lodge because it was something that I always had a bag of in the back of my truck.

One main topic that we talked about was the energy in the old residential school. After breakfast was served, we went to do the Cleansing Ceremony. There were a few people who were going to do the ceremony, and the Grand Mother wanted everyone else to form a circle around the sacred fire and pray for us all. She only wanted all the elders and my fire keeper to come with us during this time. The fire keeper came because the fire needed to be lit outside the residential school for the Cleansing Ceremony. I was forty-four years old at that time and felt honored to be asked to be one of the elders at the Elders Medicine Wheel Society. They always talked about how they wanted my sister and me to sit on the board of directors of the society.

The fire keeper had some cedar wood all cut up for the ceremonial fire that was built in front of the old residential school. We lit the fire, drummed and prayed as we started going into the old dorms of the residential school. It was a three-story building with a staircase at each end. One end was a dorm for boys and the other for girls. We started at the bottom, going through all the rooms and dorms. After we smudged two floors, we started going up the stairway toward the third floor. Halfway between the floors, my fire keeper got startled and screamed at the top of his lungs. He shook violently like a leaf in a strong windstorm. You could feel the energy on the third floor. A few of us continued on as our sister took care of the fire keeper. You could really feel the energy of the spirits as we started to smudge. The main elder told us to leave the fire for now under the circumstances and go and check on our brother who got startled. The medicine wheel was a good place to do work and everyone tried to help the young man who was still having a hard time. The fire keeper mentioned that his room was up there and that the little rooms were where the priests stayed. You don't want to know what went on up there. It wasn't a pretty picture.

We had a sweat for the young man who had a bear scratch him down his back in the western doorway, but all I could think about was going mushroom picking. The whole weekend became quite stressful, and when it came time to set my rock down ahead of the rock I set last year, I drove up to the Zoo, which was what they called the Mushroom Camp near Kitwanga, BC.

THE ZOO

Whenever I traveled near Burns Lake, I would visit my old friend who was our benefactor's ex-husband. He lived with his partner in a small log cabin on the edge of a huge lake near Mount Nadina, which towered toward the heavens. I always loved seeing Mount Nadina. It had to be one of the best views of a mountain close to the coastal mountain range. Many stories went through my mind like a projector. Then there was the pine-cone picking job, which was one of the best jobs ever. In 1987, I lived in that area and got the job picking pine cones that freshly fallen off pine trees on the slopes of Mount Nadina. At that time, we made $250 a day, which to me was good money for a day's work, especially because I was used to living on $8,000 a year. This made me happy, which was all I ever wanted. To get by and go to Mexico in the winter.

I better tell you a short story about an old neighbor friend who homesteaded the area in the early 1900s. There was an old Indian trail from Huston, BC, to an early settlement near Wisteria. He would take a wheel barrel and walk approximately ninety miles to town, load the wheelbarrow with as many supplies as possible and walk the old Indian trail back to his homestead. Hearing stories like these have always been my life long journey of its own.

I want to tell you about my best bear story before we continue on to the Zoo. I stopped at my friend's place to eat some fresh-caught char from his lake. One morning, I walked up to see the view. My friend warned me to be careful of an old black bear eating huckleberries in the area. I took the easiest trail available from the driveway, which twisted up toward the sunrise and the main road. My heart sang as I walked toward the light and the huge lake with trumpeter swans. In the light of the new day with snow-covered mountain in Tweedsmear Park, there stood a caribou herd that foraged for food. To my right was my favorite view of Mount Nadina in all her glory, shimmering in a pink light of the new morn. After I sat to do my morning prayers, I began to walk back down the rutted driveway toward my friend's cabin. I was just about there when I needed to go around this very sharp curve that was lined by Saskatoon berry bushes. I took a very sharp left turn, while, at the same time, the old black bear turned right. We met face to face. I automatically screamed with out stretched arms. For some reason, it was an automatic reflex that I had gone over in my mind as I had walked many miles in bear country. It was an amazing experience. No, I didn't need toilet paper, but very close. To my amazement it worked. The loud scream from deep fear scared the bear off, which made it turn around and run off in the opposite direction. I was frozen to the spot and shouted for my friend who was already coming up the driveway with a gun in hand. He said that I didn't have to call and that he heard my screams of terror and came running.

My mind was on the Zoo. What was I getting myself into, I thought, as I pulled out of my friend's driveway. It was only about a five-hour drive from where he lived. I was early, but I liked it that way because I could go get myself familiar with the country and the people before I went to see the chief to ask him about going on their land.

I finally arrived at the site of the famous Zoo Pine Mushroom Camp that was situated outside of Kitwanga, BC. I saw camps made out of plastic tarps with "Café" written on them, while others had "Buyers" signs and grocery stores. It seemed that everything was all set up and ready for the pickers to come with their eyes glowing in dollars and stories of last year's episodes of the Zoo.

The Zoo was like an old Gold Rush mining town. Someone mentioned that the Winnebago was the first to set up camp. People came early to get good campsites. They knew the ropes because they had come for years. The Winnebago was the local whorehouse. Yes, you read right. I said there was everything, including a man who came to pick mushrooms and set up a church for Sunday services in his plastic cathedral. Almost everyone had a gun of some sort, especially the buyers because they paid in cash and would have thousands of dollars on hand at any given point. The camp was about fifty miles from the closest town one way, and the other way was many miles up the Stewart-Cassiar Highway. One good thing about this camp was really good water that ran by in a large, rocky creek. I had to go up to the Iskut area, which was a long way when you drove an old 1973 Fargo half pickup with a Slant Six motor. Personally, I brought sweet grass and tobacco to ask the chief for permission to pick mushrooms on his land. It just happened that the chief was going out to his own summer camp in the bush along with some Grand Mothers and Grand Fathers. We journeyed to their camp off the beaten path and back in the forest, which was snuggled right in the trees that opened to the south for sunshine. A wall tent was set up with a campfire burning in front of it. The elders told stories from the time we got there until we went to bed. We watched the shadows dance with the trees, especially when the branches shook their leaves. The chief welcomed us to pick mushrooms on their land. The plan was to meet the parolee and the French man from Quebec. I went back to the village and got my truck to head back toward the Zoo to meet up with the two men. We met past Bell 2 on the Stewart-Cassiar highway. The French guy got in an argument in the café, and it seemed that there was previous history from other years. It got heated badly. Remember during that time there were no phones except old radios, which you could phone out on.

⁂

The year before was a bumper year. However, that year wasn't very wet so the mushrooms never came on strong. Man, were the mushroom grounds a rough go. Devil's club everywhere. Then you would find a flag, a pine mushroom that had popped out of the mossy old growth forest floor. The best ones were hidden under the moss, numerous ones that you could just see breaking out from the moss just a bit. You got on your knees and gently picked them, leaving some spores so they would grow for you the next year. That year, number ones were about seventeen dollars a pound and went up to twenty-eight dollars. It was a tough go, and we never went on the chief's territory because the mushrooms weren't showing. Tensions were high in the camp because people weren't making the money that they all hoped for. I made about $2,500, and off I went back home. At least I went home with some money.

I made my mind up, no matter what the threats were. I was not going to sign any kind of agreement that would split up the Mill Farm Cooperative with survey stakes and pavement. Other than that, all I had on my mind was the medicine wheel, Sun Dance, and pine cone/mushroom picking.

THE MEXICO DREAM

I did everything possible to save money to go to Mexico. One of the main reasons that I quit smoking was to save enough money to travel. The last time I smoked was three packs of Buckingham Plain that cost only thirty-five cents a pack. Now multiply that by three, which was enough money to travel back then. Now that I didn't drink or smoke, the savings were definitely enough to travel to Mexico. My grandkids asked why I enjoyed traveling to Mexico, and I responded, "I don't want to leave this world and say that the birds were smarter than me, so I join them every year."

I wanted to go to Mexico for the whole winter and drive my old Fargo. I spent my time getting the truck ready for the trip and packing stuff.

In my heart, I knew that the Mill Farm was over. So I didn't do much on the house, except think about Mexico. The time finally came that the old truck was ready, and so were we. Over the years I stayed with an old man down in Yelapa who had a big place that he rented out. There were hammocks to rent and a few separated sleeping quarters. There was even a communal kitchen for everyone to share. The only way to Yelapa was by boat, so we found a place to park the truck in a small seaside village, and from there we caught a panga to Yelapa. We got settled into our space and routine of going to the beach to swim every day and get fresh tortillas.

Then I had a very profound dream. The dream told me to drive north until I came to a log cabin, but everything was cement and adobe in Mexico. When I told my wife that I wanted to follow my dream, she asked if she could come, and I said, "Sure."

So off we went back to get our truck and head up north.

The truck was a little dusty but untouched and started right up after I installed the battery. I had taken my battery out and stashed it in the back of my truck. It was the one thing I was worried about because those old trucks had no hood locks and anyone could pop the hood to grab the battery easy.

So we headed north toward Tepic. We parked the truck in Tepic to have a taco at a little café. When we returned to the truck, there was a policeman with our license plate in his hand. He told me that I was parked in the wrong place, but he couldn't show me a sign that stated the fact. Before I could get my plate back, I had to give him a bribe. He had us over a barrel, so I paid him what he asked for, which was around twenty Canadian dollars.

I decided to secure the license plates with some different bolts that would be very hard to remove without special tools. As we drove north, the road went from pavement to gravel, then to a washed-out rutted trail with no bridge, where you had to drive through the creek beds. Everyone we talked to said, in Spanish, that it was very dangerous and would point their fingers to the side of their head like a gun.

We didn't go very far, and there was a line of Mexicans standing across the road to block our path. They said that there was a truck over the side of the road and to be careful. I was so afraid that they were going to rob us. As we were about to drive away, they mentioned that it was going to be very dangerous, for there were bandits ahead. One has to remember that we drove an old truck and didn't have any cameras, and there was no electronic equipment with us. One thing that I did have was a long machete under my seat, just in case. We never saw any ranch until it got dark. A man came running and opened the gate where we pulled off. He spoke a different language than Spanish or English. We figured out what he was saying and pulled up real close to the *casa* so that we would be safe.

We had the best supper ever. All we had was fresh fried eggs and one little square of meat along with fresh corn tortillas. Everything tasted so real to our taste buds. Even the small amount filled you with the taste of love. They had two small children who would giggle every time we spoke. It was so cute to hear the children's laughter.

What a way to travel. I felt like right out of a time capsule. All I knew was that we had to go north and find a log cabin. During our drive that day, we saw burned-out cars and trucks on the side of the road and some suspicious-looking guys that would cruise by us giving us the eye. One of our saving graces was to pick up anyone walking along the side of the road. There was a group of Native Indians that lived in the area, not the Huichol, who also spoke a different dialect. We went through one town called Jesus in the middle of nowhere, and there was no one at all on the streets. We bought a few things and went on our way. As night fell, we wondered what we were going to do. There was no way that we wanted to park on the side of the road. So when we saw the first ranch, we stopped at the gate, and sure enough a man came out and said to come on in. We pulled up real close to the house. They wanted to give us their bed. They spoke Spanish, so we had a good conversation. I told them about my dream, and they said that they had never heard of a log cabin before. After having supper and breakfast along with a packed lunch, we hit the road heading north. It actually became a real gravel road. As the road turned into pavement, we could see a large village in the distance. It was a Huichol village; you could sure tell because all the Indians were dressed in ceremonial Huichol dress of colorful fabrics, hats, and beads.

I could see that the land rose up high to the north, which was the Sierra Madre mountain range. In my dream, the log cabin was up high in the mountains. So off we went in that direction, toward the high plateau. As we drove, I kept looking for a road that went toward the mountain but never came across a road. Was I on a wild goose chase? In my dream, it said high up to the north I would find the log cabin. I began to think that my mind was starting to play tricks on me. Oh a road block, now what? We knew that there were areas that no tourists were allowed into because the government never wanted tourists to go into the old Huichol communities at all. The military men who walked on over to our truck came from behind a stack of sandbags and carried huge guns that looked like machine guns. Right away they asked, in Spanish, how we got there. My wife and I tried to tell them and all they did was look at one another with strange expressions. So I took out a piece of paper and drew a map of where we came from. We were on the other side of their road blocks, and they were very confused as to how we could have gotten there. They knew we could never have gotten through their road blocks. They finally understood after scratching their heads in disbelief. After talking to one another, they had no choice but to believe us. After they searched the truck and asked a lot of questions about all my medicines that I carried, including my pipe and sacred tobacco. Since many of the military personnel were indigenous, they were very interested in us and told us that we could go.

Soon after we left the military checkpoint, we saw a horse's skull in the ditch. Kimi wanted it so we grabbed the horse's skull, which was all bleached clean by the sunshine. Right away I felt we were in the wrong place. I wanted to be on the top of that mountain that was coming closer in my rearview mirror. We stopped and asked an old man, and he said that the road was a main road, which it felt like to us. I pointed to the tall mountain and he told us to go back and down a road at a sign that was called Autun. So we turned around and fifteen minutes came to the military personnel that were a different crew. None of them had seen us before and said that we weren't allowed to go through here. No one was allowed but residents. It was really hot, and I asked one of them if he wanted a drink. He said yes, and that broke the ice. We talked for a long time, and in our broken Spanish told him the story of my dream. The man was an indigenous person. We talked for over an hour and finally he said, "OK." He needed to ask the sergeant from the last watch if he remembered us, and away he went. After a short wait, he came back and told us that he shouldn't do this, but he was going to let us to go through. Wow! I started to think we didn't have a chance. Thank goodness they were from the original people of this land, Mexico.

Away we went. We turned at the road, and there looked to be a small *pueblo* off to the side. It was like they had radar because we drove a short distance, and there was seven big men standing firm in the middle of the road. They were of Spanish descent, so we talked and they introduced themselves. What we realized was that this was no village; it was a farm that probably had been here for four hundred years, and they were all of the same family.

They said, "Sure, you can go across our land and after ten kilometers, you will meet a gravel road. Turn left, and it will take you up the mountain." The road wasn't a road. It was more of a grass trail through their farm. Halfway through, we came across another small village, which was probably another farm. There were houses only a lane apart from one another. The people stood looking like we were Martians. We just waved and kept going. We hit the gravel road and turned left, went for a few miles, and saw a burned-out church that was very old. Then in the distance, we saw a rundown-looking *pueblo* with dirt streets, and past the village we saw a road twisting up the hill toward the high plateau. Still, no log building; however, there was a store with not many things at all for sale. Must had been a very poor village. As we left the town and turned up the winding road, there was an old log cabin sitting in the sun on its own. Yeah, I couldn't believe my eyes, either, a log cabin. We just kept driving upward on the steep hill and saw the biggest Kinnikinnick plant that I had ever seen. Got back into the truck and now, five days after the dream, I still needed to go beyond. The feeling was like going to a different planet as we hit the top. It was a flat cornfield as far as you could see. Off to the left, there was a small cornstalk house on stilts with a grass roof, which was something I had never seen or heard of before. As we drove farther on the old trail, we saw a whole group of Huichol people working. They all wore ceremonial dress, which we later learned wasn't ceremonial dress; it was what they wore all the time. Again people stood across the road. They sure never wanted anyone to speed past them. A young man came forward and spoke a different language—the original language of Huichol. We did sign language for a while, and I had some gifts that we offered to them. Then an old woman came up and did the old look-in-the-eye routine for some time. She called the young man up and said something to him, and everyone stepped aside to welcome us to their land.

We only drove a little way and pulled over to get our thoughts. We looked over the hill at a small *colonia.* There were only a few buildings that looked like schools and municipal buildings. An old man came running toward us from the small home on the ridge. He asked us to stay at his house. We couldn't understand a word he was saying, but we got the message. So we drove into his yard, which was alive with farm animals. He said it was a full moon, and all the men would go to the hills to do peyote. As I write, I wonder how we ever understood all of this, but we did. In my hand gestures, he understood that I didn't want to leave my wife. We learned later that the men of this *colonia* would go every full moon to do the Peyote Ceremony, which they had done since the beginning of time.

The children came home from school, and we had a lot of fun with learning their language through hand signals. Laughter was always in the air. The houses were built out of corn stalks and were very small. They seemed to be used only for sleeping. When the blankets that were used as the door were pushed to the side, you could see blankets on the floor. The kitchen was outside with a fire pit being the main focal point. There were a few empty boxes sitting around that were used for seats.

After a good night's sleep, we went down to the *colonia.* There were a couple of food stores and one craft store that looked like it was a local kind of cooperative. We later learned that it was where the locals brought their crafts to and then sent to some dealer in Puerto Vallarta, Mexico. The building that looked like some kind of government building was actually the health center. We met the doctor and nurse. The doctor was able to speak English, Spanish, and Huichol. Yeah! Someone we could talk to. He said we were just in time to go with one of the local men to a village in the valley down the mountain. He said it was a good day's walk. He was going to the village to get water samples because there was some cases of typhoid and that we would be welcome to go along. We wondered about the walk and decided to do it because in Yelapa all we did was walk. We thought we were in good shape. So off we went with the man in the lead. It was very evident after a little ways that we could not keep up with the doctor; he seemed to fly over the rock-strewn trail with ease. We stumbled along. We were nine thousand feet above sea level when we started and from what we could understand, we were going to the other school that was down at twenty-two hundred feet above sea level.

About halfway, the doctor got very impatient with us and told us to go over to the little hut to rest while he went down to the *colonia,* which we saw in the far distance below us. The small farm was very typical on stilts with a ramp going up to the door. The ramps were made of sticks that were set apart so that the pigs wouldn't walk up to them. It was really warm, and we learned that this was their winter home. A lot of people came down the mountain to be warmer in the winter months. The *colonia* was at the top of the mountain. It was built to have contact with the outside because it was the only place where it was possible to have a road. All the other places were where the Huichol have lived for centuries. When the Spanish Inquisition came, some areas went unseen by the Spanish because they were so far back in the mountains.

I got a fever, and we had little water. The kids had a plastic bottle and took water from the middle of the yard where all the animals drank from. They would take a scoop to see if anything squiggly was in it and dump it back into the big puddle. They did this a few times to show us. When they couldn't see anything, they drank it and handed the bottle to us. There was no way that I was going to drink that water.

The man returned from the *colonia* and was in a hurry. We mentioned that I wasn't doing too well. As I think back, it must have been the altitude. This became very apparent to me when I was twelve thousand feet up in Peru. I also got the same altitude sickness right away. We told him to go ahead and that we would find our way back. The *colonia* in the valley below didn't look too far away. He said that there was a school where we could sleep, and there was a clean river running by. After he left, we had a little talk between the two of us and decided to walk down to the *colonia*. When we arrived, there were a few ranches on the way, and as we walked by, everyone came out to see who we were and offered us a place to stay. We told them that we would go down to the school. When we got to the school, it was empty. The building had a concrete floor and that was it, an uninviting concrete floor. My wife walked down to the river for some water, which felt so good to drink. As I was trying to put it out of my mind, the man came to get water samples because there was some cases of typhoid in the *colonia.*

All the children came to see us. From our visits we knew what to do to communicate with the children. I was an old farm boy, and I loved making animal sounds from the barnyard as a youth. My first was the chicken call. All of the children would laugh, which echoed through the valley of calm. Then my wife who spoke better Spanish than I did would say "chicken" in English, then in Spanish and invite the children to say it in their language. After we would get one animal right, we would go onto the next. Once we got chickens, cows, horses, and pigs down, we would sing a song like "Old MacDonald Had a Farm" We had the time of our lives. Night came and some of the parents asked us to stay for supper and the night, but we thought we could walk back in the moonlight because I felt better. After singing another song and saying our good-byes, we started on our long walk toward the mountaintop with a full moon leading the way.

We thought that we would have no trouble walking back, but we were surprised that already after a short distance we took a wrong turn. After we had a few heated discussions, we turned around and went up the right trail. We knew that we were going the right way because we passed the ranch where the children drank out of the puddle, which was aglow in the moonlight that just broke the mountain ridge.

We were getting very tired and thought we had better stop for the night. We weren't too sure if we were going the right way. My wife started to get huge blisters, and I mean huge. I had never seen blisters so big on both of her feet.

We were on a very rocky trail, and it was hard to find any place to lie down. However, after a short distance, we found a spot where we got rocks and piled them up for a windbreak. It got very cold in the mountains. There was no snow, but we had seen ice on the puddles and frost the morning before. After the rocks were piled up, I lit a fire in front of the rocks and there was just enough room for us to lie cuddled together in order to keep warm under the full moonlight. After a very uncomfortable night, the shades of black turned into the dawn of day. We were very surprised to see our surroundings. In front of us was a very steep drop-off to the rocky valley's floor below, and above was a steep cliff.

I was feeling better, but we were very thirsty and tired due to dehydration. Before long, we saw a couple riding toward us on horses. They looked like people from 1850 instead of 1995 as they rode up to us on their horses. She rode sidesaddle, and they both wore their ceremonial dresses, but like I said we learned that these were their daily outfits. In our sign language, they told us they wanted us to come to their place, but we said we better get back because the doctor would be worried about us. As I write, I wish that I could go back there and spend more time to see where they lived. On the ground, they drew how their *colonia* was built in a circle, and the men would come to it on the full moon before they went into the mountains to do their Peyote Ceremony. I learned later that this was their spiritual *colonia,* which was built with special buildings in each direction and in the middle was an area for ceremonial purposes.

Before they rode off, we made sure that we were on the right trail. I was so thirsty, but there was no water. We did find a clear puddle of water, though, between some rocks. I never thought anything about it and just made sure there were no bugs in it. We eventually walked through an oak tree forest, which we remembered. As we cleared the forest we saw the *colonia* in the distance, our hearts sang with joy. We knew we had survived our adventure. As soon as we got close, we could hear laughter as people walked toward us. It was like the whole *colonia* came out to meet us. They were so happy to see us and know that we were safe. All we could think about was getting a Coca-Cola, which was the best for dehydration, as my wife said. Soon as we got to the store, I gulped two Cokes down and ate a bar of chocolate.

We went over to the health center to tell the doctor that we made it safe. He was apologetic for letting us go. We told him that it was our decision and it wasn't his fault. He said that his nurse knew why they had come here. I looked at him with a puzzled look. He said they had been trying for two years to heal her with no results. The problem was in her solar plexus area. He said that she had been praying and that I came into her prayers and that I was here to heal her. I was really amazed at this because I had never mentioned anything about myself. I never talked about it. I knew from my past experiences that this was how the spirit worked. It must been the reason I had the dream and the spirit was doing its work. So I told him that I needed to pray at night, and I would talk to him in the morning.

After many prayers and a good night's sleep, we walked down to the health center the next the morning. The doctor and the nurse waited anxiously for my decision. I told them that my prayers were good and that I felt good about doing this. This was the reason that I had my dream to come this way. I told him that I would only do the healing if with a woman present as a witness. The doctor asked if it was OK that he could be present. I told him that this was no problem. The woman who asked to be present looked after one of her grandchildren, so we asked my wife to look after the child instead. My wife had no problem with that.

They showed me to the treatment, and I told them that I would get ready and then call them in. I did my prayers and smudged out the whole room. I had my long roll of purple material with me, my pipe, and other medicines. I put the protection ring up and placed all the medicines in the appropriate directions. Did some final prayers and called them in. I told the nurse to lie down and for the doctor and the grandmother to stand outside the purple protection ring of material. I told them that they had to be conscious of not taking on any energy. I was told to send all of the negative energy to the other side of Mars, and use the prayers for the earth to take.

I did my personal protection prayers and began doing my deep breathing while I scanned the nurse's solar plexus area. I felt the energy within her and started talking to it in a gentle way. I told it why we were here, what we were doing, and that the bad energy couldn't stay in this host any longer. It was time for it to go on its way and leave her body free of its presence. I did my breathing in a clockwise matter and felt her discomfort as I breathed a circle over her solar plexus. I had to wait until the right time. I felt the entity was ready to leave her body. I kept praying for help from the other side. I asked for the removal of the entity to leave her body and go to the other side of Mars.

As I breathed, I spoke gently. "I'm going to pull you out and send you home in a good way." As I put my tongue on the roof of my mouth and exhaled, the entity left her body. She sat up right away and said that she hadn't felt so good in years. I was totally exhausted after this experience and packed up all my stuff. We walked home where I crashed in a lump on the bed. After a very long sleep, we went back down to the health center the next day. There was a table of gifts waiting for us, which included necklaces, beaded items, and bags. The nurse was very thankful, which she said in Spanish. One of the few things she could say. The doctor said that she felt better than ever. We kept in touch with the doctor by mail for a couple of years, and he said she was still doing well.

In the meantime, we headed back to Yelapa. When we through the military checkpoint, the soldiers again shook their heads and wondered how we got there. Away we went through Guadahara and into Puerto Vallarta to catch our panga to Yelapa. Our friends were amazed at our story and said as locals, they would not have been allowed into that area.

When we arrived home, it was still the same story about the Mill Farm trying to get us to sign the rezoning papers. We had a list of six issues, which included an environmental study. They always told us that they were working on including those issues, but we never saw any changes in their rezoning document that stated our concerns.

The medicine wheel was fast approaching, and I went over to some circle that they had in Chilliwack about planning the next wheel. When I started to set up the medicine wheel, my fireman was nowhere to be seen. When I asked about him, no one seemed to know anything about him. After the first day of setup, I was just about to turn in for the night when I heard a voice in the dark.

"Uncle, Uncle, I need to speak to you," the voice said. It was my fireman lurking in the shadows.

We sat around my fire quietly while I tried to absorb his story. I had heard a lot of people's stories over the years, but for some reason this one was an eye-opener. I realized how sexual abuse was such a bad thing to do to anyone. My fireman was a happily married man with two girls: one around six years old and the other one was twelve. I knew his family and would stay with them when I was over in Chilliwack. They were a great little family unit with much love. When he went into that residential school the year before and screamed, he was actually reliving his past. Images that day came back to him that he had somehow stuffed deep into his being and never thought could come back to haunt him. The terror of the past went through his body like a hot knife cutting deep into his soul. One of the main things I had learned as I had talked to a lot of people was that sex offenders would tell young victims that they were grooming. They would show their victim show they love them while they proceeded to abuse them.

I have no idea what went through this young man's head, but right after that experience, in the old residential school, he started to abuse his eldest daughter. At that very moment, he was being charged with abuse, which he admitted to, and his wife kicked him out. He was a very distraught young man and said he wasn't trying to hide anything and should be free to talk about this issue. However, he wouldn't be coming to the medicine wheel and wanted to let me so that I could find another fire keeper.

His story shook my whole world in so many ways because this young man had a great family in many ways. I could continue with other stories of how people had been affected by the past abuse that occurred in residential schools, but I really don't like putting that energy out into the universe because it feeds the power of the abusers.

This really made the medicine wheel hard for me. There was a lot of talk about what happened the previous year that cut deep into most people's past. This year, we had a brother come from the island who had a brain tumor and had only a week to live. We spent a lot of time working on the brother in the main circle where all the elders did their healing. He said that he felt a lot better, and he lived many years after that medicine wheel. My friend Jason was a quad, and he was going to come to the Pine Mushroom Camp after the medicine wheel. We got him drinking juniper tea, which tasted strong, but tasted even better when mixed with mint tea. After two days of drinking this tea, he started to get a feeling in one of his legs.

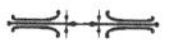

People were really interested in hearing about my Sun Dance experiences, except for the Grand Mother. For instance, I started using one of the brothers who was on the ETA pass from the local prison. He had been on the inside for over thirty years and was interested in the teachings that I shared with him. He said that he wished that I could come into the jail and share a sweat lodge ceremony with them. They started to get the sweats set up in the local federal prisons and introduced me to the head of Aboriginal Programs for all the local prisons. The man told the head that he wished that they had someone like me to do sweats on the inside. There was a court decision that gave aboriginal offenders the same rights as other prisoners. Other prisoners had their religious leaders come into the jail to offer services, like the Catholics, Anglicans, and other mainstream religions. This new law allowed people to come share the sweat lodge ceremony inside the razor fences.

I had no idea what was in store for me because my dreams would never had dreamed such a dream.

All I could think about was going up north to the mushroom patch. I had already talked with the chief. After the closing ceremony, which was amazing this year, most people saw hundreds of spirits float across the field in a mist of gray. I had never seen so many spirits at once. Because they came on the closing day, it seemed like they were telling us that we were doing the right thing. Many people died violently in those residential schools. There are many horror stories, even about newer buildings built over the unmarked graves of many residential children. Some of the stories also told of young girls who got pregnant by their abusers and suddenly disappeared.

I left as soon as I could in order to head north to the Mushroom Camp. I always stayed around the hundred-mile house to leave early in the morning before sunrise, which I witnessed coming over the hills in the south of Williams Lake. This made my heart soar whenever I saw this spectacular scene. During the night, I had an amazing dream of wolves. The Grand Mother always said she used the wolf as her messenger. We are taught to remember which way the animal came into our dreams and what direction it left. The two wolves were looking over their backs to the north as they headed into the southern direction.

For the whole day, I kept going over my dream. I was excited about to get there because the chief invited me to his house; it felt great to be able to freely pick on their land. I stopped just outside Kitwanga, which was pretty close to my destination. During that night, I had another dream. It was in the old porch of the house we lived in outside of Hoadley. The porch faced east and in the south end of the porch there was my father-in-law trying to sweep some newborn mice into a box. He would try very gently to sweep them in, but they would just escape again out of holes in the cardboard box. Man, this dream really drove me nuts again to the south and the determination of the mouse. Over my morning coffee, all I did was pray for the direction, and all that came to me was that I had to go south. Did something happen at home? What was with all these dreams? Both of them were telling me to go south. So I phoned the chief to let him know that I was going home because of these two dreams. He understood, so instead of going north, I turned around to go south. During my drive back, all I could do was pray and ask for guidance. I missed the last ferry and during the night had another dream. While I was asleep in the back of my truck, I waited for the ferry booth to open the next morning. I was in a small cabin on a couch when all of a sudden a grizzly bear busted in the front door, which opened into a small space. My grandmother stood up on the couch and sung to the bear. The bear came up to me and put his paw on my head ever so gently. Then it looked straight into my eyes and turned around to go out through the door. Wow! What a dream sequence. I finally understood my dreams. Now I knew what the Grand Mother's Indian name meant. It meant "Grand Mother Grizzly Bear," and she needed me. She had sent the wolves as the messenger and now the grizzly bear. She put her heart-side hand on the person's head when she worked on people.

When I awoke from my dream, it was time to get on the first ferry. I will always remember this day, for it was a Sunday. My wife was surprised to see me, and I told her about my dreams. When I told her the last one, she asked if I would be gone for a long time.

I told her that I was catching the first ferry the next day Monday to Chilliwack. I had to be a foot passenger because I had little money to take the truck over.

When I got to Chilliwack, there were a lot of cars at the Grand Mother's healing lodge parking lot and a fire going outside.

When I arrived, she was so happy to see me. "I have been sending you my prayers. I knew you would come, my boy." I was just in time to join their circle. It was as if the spirit had written out the timeline for me.

The society had hired a helper for the healing project who went inside the prisons. The project was to work with the Native brothers and sisters who were in jail serving federal time for two years plus a day. Why a lot of people got sentenced to a federal, but the offender can also receive some programming, which the Provincial system doesn't offer. The female helper was hired as a coordinator for the Medicine Lodge Society. The circle was fairly big, containing ten people, most of whom I had met. Right off the bat, I caught the gist of what was going on. She didn't like who the group had hired to work with her. This was a woman with the right credentials to do the job, who they hired through the interview process. However, the Grand Mother was upset with how the woman presented herself to the correctional staff and the inmates when they went inside to interview the brothers. She wanted to fire the lady on the spot, especially after the feather was passed to the woman and she just passed it without saying a word. When the feather came to some of the main people who hired her, they said that they couldn't just let her go, that it didn't work that way in today's world.

When the feather came back to the Grand Mother, she said, "I'm firing her." Especially since the woman had refused to take the feather. The woman was obviously very upset and really had no idea what she got herself into. She did take the feather after and said in a choking voice that she understood the Grand Mother's concern about her not knowing any of the teachings, and that she was an academic and not a healer. She was willing to step aside and let the Grand Mother hire someone more to her liking. Then the feather went to the Grand Mother and she said that she wanted me, Bruce, to do the job because I knew the teachings and would be a good fit to go inside the prison.

When the feather came to me, I said, "I never had a job as a coordinator and would have a hard time doing all the paperwork and thought I had better pass it on." I passed the feather on and the Grand Mother was persistent.

She said, "I want Bruce to have this job, and I know that he can do it." So I took the job as the coordinator for the Medicine Lodge Society. I knew my wife wouldn't be happy about my decision.

When I told her, she said, "See, I told you you would be gone a long time following that dream."

I had a little office space that had all the society's papers in it. The papers included how the society was formed and cooperation registry as a public society. One of the main reasons for this was so that people could get a tax break when they gave a donation. It was a great job in many ways. I even took the Grand Mother to events and meetings everywhere. She was the elder at a lot of schools and universities or many of the local Indian bands functions, and her calendar year was always full. There never seemed to be a day off. Then there were always invites to the local federal institutions. One of the first things that I had to do was get security clearance to go inside the local jails, which I did with no problems.

I soon learned a lot about how this society was formed and that it was on the Grand Mother's land, which was on the reserve where she lived. It was a very valuable piece of land comprised of eight acres of farmland in the middle of the Fraser Valley. Having had limited companies myself, I knew that there were forms that needed to be kept up to date. The society was always overdue with their paperwork being submitted to the society's board in Victoria.

While I was at home, I thought to stop into their office in Victoria. When they showed me what was needed, I saw three names crossed out on the form. She mentioned that I one of the main reasons that she need this information was because someone had sent these forms in and crossed out the Grand Mother's name and two of the other main directors of the company. This was strange to me as to why this had happened. Back in Chilliwack, I showed her the paper and asked her what she knew about it. She, too, was shocked because she couldn't understand how that could happen. Since the Companies Act office had these papers, it meant that we had to fill out new forms to get them back on the list of society directors. No one would come forward with any information as to why this was done or who could have scratched these three names off the registry. Well, I guess that was one of the main reasons that I had those dreams and followed them. At the end, by following my dreams, it saved her society and her land.

The prisons were a lot of fun, and we would get some of the offenders out to speak to children in a circle at the local schools. My stomach at the time started to grow every day, it seemed; there was always a lot of food around, and you always had to be stuffing your face to show your gratitude.

Corrections gave me a course, which made me an escort. This meant that I could escort prisoners on their escorted time passes. At first, we worked a lot with minimum security prisons, but they soon wanted us to go into all of them, including the maximum prison. The only prisoners that could get escorted time passes were the ones in minimum institutions. At this time, there was a lifer that was in a minimum, and he had asked to go to his brother's funeral in Alberta. I was surprised when they asked me to escort him. I learned later that this was the first time a citizen escort ever escorted a prisoner out of the province for a few days. So here I am with this huge tattooed man getting on an airplane to Alberta. They even gave me a car rental as well as a lot of money for food and hotel. What happened was every night at nine, I had to have the inmate checked into the local jail, in Alberta. In the daytime we visited his family, which was a lot of fun with. They were so happy to see their loved one.

When the last day came, I said, "I have one hundred and twenty dollars left that needs to be spent." Everyone wanted KFC, so we got on the phone to order. Remember this was twenty years ago, which equals a lot of chicken. They drove us crazy. KFC phoned at least three times to check to make sure it was no joke that we ordered so much chicken. I had never seen so much chicken. Made me think of Jim Morrison. I started to realize that the corrections people had a lot of faith in me to use me as a citizen escort. This meant that they never had to spend money on their own staff to do this.

One of my tasks was to submit papers for funding to different government agencies. They had me go to workshops in order for me to learn to do this. I got very tired of doing this job because I was away from home so much, and the ferry fees gave me an empty wallet. I would finish work on Friday and rushed to the ferry to get home late at night. I only spent one day then left early on Sunday morning to catch the ferry again to go back to work.

My head was in the clouds in many ways. I never thought much about the Mill Farm these days. In my mind, it was gone anyway, so I gave little attention to the cooperative. In some ways, I just wanted it gone—then the waiting game would be over. I thought they thought that I would sign the papers. If they waited long enough, I would had come to my senses and sign their rezoning application that would put feathers in the hats of local politicians. I still don't know why I was so stubborn, but I was and didn't want to change my mind.

I got very tired of going back and forth for the job and taking care of the old Grand Mother. It was an interesting job, but it was sure strange in the society. I always wondered why someone would scratch those names off, which got the better of me sometimes.

There was talk that a developer wanted to give the Grand Mother a deal and build a gated community on her reservation land. If it had happened, then that would mean a lot of money, but it was something she didn't want to do. She was happy just leasing to a local farmer who grew root crops. In the legal documents of the society, they controlled the whole piece of property, and it was controlled by the founding elders. If someone was to get in there to replace three first names with others, they would have controlled the whole eight acres with the lodge and the Grand Mother's house on it.

At times I got tired of the sedentary lifestyle, sitting around in meetings and driving a lot. Especially when we had to drive all the way into Vancouver for some meetings.

One day, I went into sweats at a medium-security institution with the guys. Sometimes when their institutional elder wasn't there, they would ask me if I would do a sweat for them. The only way they could have a sweat was to have someone from the outside do it; otherwise it sat there vacant.

I continued to get tired of being the coordinator and asked the Grand Mother to hire someone else because I knew my work was finished and I had done what she asked me. I completely straightened up the books and put them in order. I went through those filing cabinets over and over. I knew everything in them by heart.

The time had finally came. "Sign or be taken to court," they said.

I said, "Take me to court." That was the time when the artists' and writers' group got into full gear. We tried to raise funds through auctions to raise money in order to buy the Mill Farm. All I could think about was getting away from my coordinator position, which had turned into an office job. Yet the best part of the whole thing was working with the boys. I got my son to go to the court case for me, which was set for December—a perfect time for us to go to Mexico.

Afterward, I told the Grand Mother of my situation and that I wanted to quit. She got upset and didn't want me to leave. I told her that I never worked a nine-to-five job and needed a break anyway. So I gave my two weeks' notice, and she told me just to go. At the last meeting, in the prison, I told the guys that I had to leave, and it was nice to have worked with them.

Right after, I got a message to meet with the head of Aboriginal Programs from Corrections Canada that was at the regional headquarters in Abbotsford, BC. *What could this be about?* I thought to myself. Since I was still over there I decided to meet with them. It was a huge secure building in Abbotsford. I was used to the security, and everywhere you went you had to show your identification. When I went up the stairs to meet with them, I was surprised at how many people worked for the government. There were offices and desk areas everywhere I looked. I'm glad that I sat down when I heard what they were about to ask me. They began by saying that they wanted to ask me this before, but they never did because they had talked to the Grand Mother, who said no. So now that they had learned that I had quit my position as the coordinator for the Medicine Lodge Society, they wanted to offer me a position. They had heard very good reports about my services, especially from some of the members who had sat in the sweat lodge with me. The brotherhoods had also said that they really liked the teachings that had been handed down to me, and they felt comfortable in the sweat lodges with me. So what they wanted to offer me was a contract to work under the regional Native elder as his apprentice, and that I would work into the position of an elder when the first position as an elder came up at a local prison. I was dumbfounded. In my wildest dreams, I never thought this would ever be a possibility. I sat there thinking to myself, not saying a word for a while.

I said, "I work for the spirit and not a paycheck. I want to take a break from everything and go away to Mexico for a while, when I return, I will give you my answer." They looked at one another, puzzled. I guess they thought I would say yes. One of the main things I needed to do was pray and talk to some of my teachers. So we left it at that as we shook hands, and I walked out the door to freedom.

When I got outside I pinched myself to see if I was alive and not dreaming. This was just a huge offer and the money that was offered was much more than I had ever made anywhere except the days that I farmed in Hoadley. Really, what was on my mind besides Mexico was the fact that we were taught not to take money for our services that came from the spirit.

When I got home and told my wife, she was very happy that I quit but didn't know what to think about the new offer. All that was on my mind was, you guessed it, Mexico. I figured this was all my grandmother's doing. When I was seven years old, she took my sister and me down to my Uncle Bruce's home in Chula Vista, California, by bus from Calgary, Alberta. It was a three-day trip on the bus. I really remember orange groves everywhere. The bus stopped at the roadside stands, and I always wanted an orange for they tasted so good. I also remembered going to Tijuana, Mexico, which was just a bunch of tin shacks and a market place. The little crocodiles that were on sale mesmerized me. I wanted one bad, but I knew it was out of the question. Everywhere a seven-year-old's eyes look is wonderment of life and color. When I talked to my sister about this a couple of years back, she said that Grandmother never told Uncle Bruce that we were coming. She just got us on a bus, and away we went. There was a story about how she cashed in some kind of savings fund and thought this would be a good thing to do with the money. My grandmother was wise beyond words. Her educational practices still amaze me in many ways. When I think about, the best education you can get is to travel and talk to the elders. Writing this, I just realized in the moment that she began to teach me that at seven years old. That's probably the main reason why I wanted to take all our kids to Mexico. After they graduated, we went to Mexico in order to learn about another culture. I always joked that I wanted to take them on their graduation because it gave me an excuse to go to Mexico. I also told my sister that I had never been to Las Vegas. And she mentioned that I had gone when we went on that bus trip with Grandmother, and we stopped in Las Vegas. So whenever any of my poker-playing buddies ask if I have ever been to Las Vegas, I say yes, in 1954. This always got me a few comments when I said this.

At least I had a bit of money saved up for the trip this time to Mexico, and it was easier loading up the old truck, for I had some experience from the prior year. The great thing about taking the truck was that I could bring stuff back, especially things like blankets, because I was getting stuff together for my four-year giveaways even though it was a couple of years away yet.

We figured that we would go the 5 Freeway route, which was real easy because there was only one traffic light between Canada and Mexico. We would go through the Nogales border to cross Mexico after stops at the four corners and places along the way, like Mesa Verde.

It felt like home as soon as we hit Yelapa. Everyone greeted us like family, and my old buddy had his horses there to take our stuff up to our *casita* on the hill, which overlooked the bay toward the Marieta Islands. The panga trip was always exciting at that time. A huge manta ray went right under our panga with its rays showing on each side of the boat. Their span was about sixteen feet. There were always dolphins jumping along with a few swordfish and whales that were always a sight to see. This was the year that there was a huge earthquake that hit Los Angeles and knocked a lot of overpasses down. My son was there with my granddaughter, and as we were walking down the beach in Yelapa, we felt the earth shake. You could see it wave like a carpet flipping. The vibration was so effective that our granddaughter fell facedown on the beach. Thank goodness she had a blanket of sand to land on. It's funny how your body senses go through different feelings when the energy of a quake is upon you. It was just the day before that we got word about my son's friend who had taken his own life. He, too, was just like a son to me. It was really hard to get any messages at that time in Yelapa. There was only an old radio phone in one of the houses, but the family wanted us to know and asked if I could come home and do the ceremony. A good friend of ours who was down in Mexico said he would pay for our flights back and that he would come back with us for the service. So we got everything together to head back to Canada. Since he was a comic, he wanted to stop over in LA to hit an improv comedy club that was very famous. I never thought about this until much later, but I think our friend took his life for many reasons. I don't want to get into that here, but it was just after the court case. I always had a hard time with this topic because I knew the story so well. One day before we left for Mexico, this young man said to me that I had been present for every good moment that he had in his life. Man, that made me feel so good to hear this story from him. The part I knew about was the fact he made a deal with his friend who also was a quad but ended up being able to walk, which was an amazing story by the way. They made a deal when they met in the hospital in Vancouver. The deal was if either one of them ever wanted to end his life, the other one would help. At first, I thought, *Oh well*, but as time passed, I had a hard time with that fact. If they never had this agreement, would my friend who was like a son to me be here today?

We headed to the airport in Puerto Vallarta and back to L.A. for a night's stopover. Our friend never partied at home, but when he went south, he sure made up for it. It was a night to remember. The improv club sure was fun; most of the comic routines were about the earthquake, which was still embedded in people's minds as it was just the other day. We saw damage everywhere we went in L.A. After the club, we went down to Venice Beach and to a bar for our friend to get drinks. There we met a street person who wanted to show us his world, which he did. The first thing he showed us was how he lived in the trunk of an old car that was parked on the street. We never looked in the trunk because he never wanted to get any attention. He said he would quickly hop into the trunk of this car unnoticed and got a good night's sleep. He took us around and introduced us to all his friends in the hood, including an area where people stood around a barrel that had a fire in it. We never felt at risk during this time that we walked among homeless people.

Then we met one of his friends, and he said, "We have something that we would like to share with you. It's not pot; it's opium. Would you like to try it?" I said sure. I had heard about it and was willing to try anything once. So here we were, downtown in L.A., smoking opium out of a bullet made into a pipe as the sun rose over the Pacific Ocean. It was a great feeling to relax the body right away, which made you feel at ease within yourself. Before we knew it, we had to rush to the airport to our connecting flight to Vancouver.

The ceremony was a happy event to honor the life of our good friend. In the back room at the hall, many people got a rose tattoo. We did a ceremony where we all cut our hair and offered it to the fire outside. I wanted to light the fire. One of the best things was when someone drove our friend's Harley into Beaver Point Hall in order for our friend to ride it into his new journey. All this made it real easy for me to say my peace. Now our young friend would journey alongside us in a different way. Well, when I get to the other side, the first thing that I'm going to do is give that young man a big hug. I say that now, but I never said that at first.

After the ceremony and many hugs, we headed right back to Mexico. We never put any energy into any talk about losing the Mill Farm because it was all about our friend's ceremony of life.

We had to get back to Yelapa because one of our kids was flying down for a graduation present. When the kids came down, we always rented a boat and took them to the Marietas where the blue-footed booby lived. The Bay of Banderas was a huge old volcano and the Marietas were on the edge of it, a two-hour panga ride from Yelapa. There were caves there that you can drive a semi through. That's how big they were and you could still walk all over the island, but now they are protected and have one of the best coral reefs for scuba diving. One of the biggest highlights of our trip was catching fish and making fresh ceviche, which tasted so good. After scuba diving and walking through the caves, we went to beaches where there were no people on them.

Our time was up. I was a bit worried because the plates of our truck had expired, and I never said a word about this because we never had much money to get home. So off we went. I was really worried about stopping at the Mexican border because we did fly out. It amazed me how we did that because you were not supposed to leave a vehicle in Mexico if you had drove one down. So I was a bit nervous about the fact that we had already left the country and now we were leaving again, but we sailed right by the Mexican border with no problems. Thought this wasn't the case on the American side. Not the same story at all, and they put us through it majorly. One of the main reasons was because we had a home-made camper on the back of the old truck, which also had been remodeled a lot in the cab of the truck. In the back of the truck, the first thing you saw were black garbage bags, a few of which held dirty laundry. It was a female customs officer who told us to park to the side. When she and the other officers came over to inspect the truck, I had to open the back because they couldn't figure it out. I had a secret locking system that they couldn't figure out, so they asked me to open it for them. They had us standing to the side. It seemed that they didn't want us near the truck when they searched it. Maybe it was the smell of the laundry or some of my medicines, but they only looked inside and quickly closed the back.

They said, "OK, on your way, have a safe trip."

We had no money left, so I had to use an old trick. It worked then, but don't know if it would work today. It was kind of like how I would survive when I was a kid on the road in 1962. I would be going through a town like Kamloops, BC, and go to the local police station and tell them I had no money or a place to stay. They would tell me a place to go and always said to be out of town by ten in the morning, which was the deal. A lot of times I also got meal tickets for a local café, sometimes even food vouchers. If there was no place to stay, they would put you up in their lockup, feed you, and let you out with a meal ticket at the local greasy spoon, which they were called at the time.

USING AN OLD TRICK

So I learned to do this in the States. I would stop at the highway patrol office and tell them my hard-luck story, and they would give me a gasoline ticket. They would even give me some advice about where we could find a local food bank that gave out food and just tell them that the officers had sent us. We kept north toward the border and went all the way to the border doing this. No one even noticed my plates were expired, even my wife.

When we finally got home after eating nothing but ninety-nine-cent American hamburgers, we were very surprised to see a notice on our door on our mountain home. It was the Capital Regional District telling me that we had to be out the March 17. It was March 15 when we arrived home. We learned that they sent the CRD inspector here with the building inspector on March 10 in order to inspect the buildings, which weren't theirs until March 17. This seemed like they were forcing us out because they wanted our home to use as a cottage for a caretaker for their new Mill Farm Park.

Why weren't we given a chance to be the caretakers when we knew every square inch of the mountain? There was a precedent that had been set because we had been the caretakers for years. Before we lived here, people used to shoot stuff up and steal lumber and building supplies. Some of our old partners used to be happy that we where there on the mountain.

How do Robert Bateman, Carol Evans, Carol Hag, and Mountain Co-op—who donated thousands of dollars—feel about the way we were being treated and the fact that CRD had decided to tear down our house, which had been grandfathered and was the spirit of this land?

In the old days, they would shoot you if you didn't move. Today, they slowly take away all your dignity until you don't have the strength to fight anymore. This ended up with my family splitting and us being on welfare, which was a sad state of affairs. This felt the same way that we were treated by our old partners. My mind still went over it, especially seeing the documents that hung on our home's door, which we built with love from our hearts.

We never received a copy of this letter that was sent to us because we were in Mexico. It was a legal document because it was their land legally on March 17, which was only two days away. My wife was going crazy because it stated that all the buildings and personal chattels on the lands became the new owner's property. There was no way in God's green earth that I could possibly move everything off the mountain in two days. We were very tired from our journey through the States. Like I said, my mind couldn't help but think. If the original mandate had been followed, the real estate transactions wouldn't have occurred, and the Partition Act wouldn't be in front of the courts.

I knew it would happen sooner or later. Some new guy who bought a share would want to capitalize on his investment.

LOST OUR DREAM

The loss of the case resulted in a forced sale of our property. Being as our property contained one of the highest remaining concentrations of old-growth Douglas fir on the island, a logging company was sure to be one of the bidders. I couldn't help but wonder if the petitioners had bought into our co-ownership agreement according to the original mandate that they would have a true representation of the Mill Farm Cooperative. They must have been accepted by the group and would have understood the basic concept of the co-ownership agreement instead of buying into an alternative community. This was hard for a real estate agent to understand. We wouldn't have to go before the courts if our Mill Farm agreement was followed. I felt that I had to make a stand for the simple fact that the trust had not been given a true copy of legally documented bylaws describing the co-ownership agreement in full past and present.

Had we been able to buy them out, or locate like-minded investors, we could have avoided the courts. Unfortunately, our luck had ran out. The judge ruled in favor of the petitioners, which meant our dream was no longer ours. The historic, spiritual, and archaeological miracle that was the Mill Farm was soon to be lost forever to the development, or so we thought, because the Pacific Conservancy was there at the court along with the group "Save the Mill Farm." The judge asked the owners who they wanted the land sold to: the loggers or the group who wanted to turn it into a park. The group chose the "Save the Mill Farm" group.

My mind still went crazy with all these thoughts as I heard my wife in the background say, "Aren't you going to do anything, or are you just going to stand there doing nothing?"

Cement Job

What was happening when we returned from Mexico was so reminiscent of the first time around, I couldn't help but think that the same players were pushing the buttons. My guess was one of these officials was talking to an old partner who held a grudge against us because they couldn't gain financially from a subdivision. There were a lot of bad vibes because we stopped the subdivision. Someone wanted to get rid of us. For the life of me, I couldn't see these officials being behind it because I had never met them and all it did was put a big black veil around a piece of Mother Earth.

As I write this, I realized that, after the court's decision, our friend who was more like a son to me took his own life with an overdose of pills. Bless his soul.

"Breathe deep, push that pulsating pain of bitterness to a different place," I told myself every day. Otherwise the razor blades scrapping in my innards were going to consume me. How could I forgive them for destroying our dream and turning our life of fourteen years into our worst nightmare? Oh well, that was another dream gone, but at least it saved the Mill Farm from the loggers.

Yet again, thanks to the "Save the Mill Farm" artists, painters, carvers, poets, and writers along with the conservancy who purchased it at the Partition Act court case.

I could hear my wife say, "Aren't you going to do something?" So I called my son who was at his house up on the mountain to go to town and pick me up a bag of Portland cement and a couple of two-by-six pieces of wood, eight feet long. When he got home, I asked him if he would mix up a batch of cement and make a wooden box out of the two-by-sixes (the box would measure three feet by three feet square with a plywood bottom). He gave me that look of "OK, what is that old man up to?" as I asked him to place it in the middle of our living room floor. Then I asked my son and his friend to move the couch over to the wooden box that sat there like a stranger in the limelight. I got on a pair of woolen socks and rubber boots and then placed my feet in the middle of the box. I sat down on the couch as I asked my son to start shoveling in the concrete. Cementing me to the house. My son and his friend shoveled the cement into the box until it was full, while giving me these crazy looks of disbelief. My wife really believed that I had finally gone over the edge of reality with this stunt. You could say that she thought I had gone over the hill and around the bend.

Once I was comfortable and the cement was dry, I called the local newspaper, the *Driftwood*; the Victoria *Times Colonist*; and the CBC. They all arrived the next day to see who the mad man was that cemented himself to his house. One reporter mentioned that this was the best assignment he had been assigned to. On the other hand, one cameraman said to his workmates, "Make this quick. I want to get back down that rough road to civilization." Instead, they ended up filling three tapes because they became so engrossed in the story. And on the first day, it became an international story, which meant that my face was on the front of every newspaper in the world. It was the first news item on television and radio stations around the globe.

Newspapers and television companies from every station sent a crew out to see who the mad man was that cemented himself to his living room and his son who helped while his wife watched. As the days ticked by, the *Times Colonist* reporter was becoming really concerned about my feet. She came up and spent the better part of every day. This was her big story, and she was covering it well. She started reading me information that said after three days of no circulation, your toes will lose all sense of feeling and have to be cut off, and maybe even your legs. She said it was like gangrene.

"Your feet are turning black right now," she said. But I told her that I wanted to hear from the CRD before I broke free of the concrete that held me like an anchor embedded into the mountainside. She was very concerned about me and would ask questions like, "How do you go to the bathroom?" Hello, what was I supposed to say? I just pointed to a plastic bucket underneath the couch. She didn't elaborate on the subject anymore.

My stomach grated like someone was rasping it clean of rust from the past. Over and over again, I thought to myself, *Was it worth it? We did save it, after all. That was a done deal*, I thought as I wiggled my toes always keeping them moving.

"Do you sleep at night sitting up like that?" she asked. It seemed that the reporter from the *Times Colonist* always had some kind of question of the day.

"What drove you to do this?" she asked.

"I told you: my wife said do something, so I did something. Doesn't get any simpler."

I said with surprise that the Capital Regional District never said anything during this time. As I sat there worrying about my feet as the hours ticked into days, I told myself every day, or otherwise the rough sandpaper that scrapped in my innards was going to consume me. How could I forgive them for destroying our dream and turning our life of fourteen years into our worst nightmare from the dark side? Who would have ever pictured that after all these years? It had gone beyond who was going to take the crap out of the outhouse to which fruit tree it would go under. As I sat there like a thinker with his elbows resting on his knees and his hands gently holding his head upward, no one could preserve the meaning of my thoughts. I guess you could say that it was what it was, folks. I sat looking out over the waters and trees of green, while I prayed that my feet wouldn't fall off.

Because my wife wasn't registered on the title as a one-tenth owner, she never had a say. This was where a lot of cooperative agreements were being figured out. The Mill Farm could have been a whole different story if the lawyer would have done it right in the first place. You have to form a legal cooperative with a book of guidelines that come with it. If that was done, we would have still be living on the mountain.

Magazine editors were showing up now. They wanted my story for their next magazine issue. I remember *BC Report* to be one of the magazines. Many people said that this was a very controversial story and that it touched on all aspects of life in today's world. It really did, in many ways, especially if you owned land with a group of people. Yet, I still felt the negative effects of the Mill Farm experience. I had to work through a lot of things over the years, but the one that still haunted me, as I sat there trying to stimulate my toes, was the betrayal of some of my best friends and partners in the Mill Farm. Changing their minds, I could understand, but the whole thing took on another turn. I became the enemy. Everyone had their sights set on approximately $250,000 if the trust got the signatures, which was what people thought it would be worth after all the development was done. I became "Salt Spring's Most Wanted Man." The bullets were words that still scare me to this day.

I wanted to save the farm. That was what we all started out to do even if a lot of our ideals were riddled with idiosyncrasies. I made a commitment to the Creator that I would never put white survey stakes in Mother Earth. I breathed deep, pushed that pulsating pain of bitterness to a different place in the universe and away from the smell of setting cement at my ankles. My thoughts were really on my quad friend who really died trying to save this land. My heart throbs a hurtful pain of knowing and understanding some of the hurtful things that he had to go through. We were at day two when all these thoughts were going through my head, while my wife just carried on with her work.

Oh my goodness, another truck story! I kid you not, it happened the first night that we got back before the cement job. My wife got a ride home just before the day she told me to do something. She took my truck to work because she sold her car for money to go to Mexico. She was so excited when her friend dropped her off on the mountain. She ran into the house saying that I wouldn't believe what had just happened. The old truck started itself. It drove right across the upper parking lot and went straight over the embankment through the patio and smashed into the patio doors where it got jammed before it came to a full stop. Then a towing company towed the truck up to Woods Garage and unhooked it in the garage's yard. I got a call from the garage early that morning at work and was asked what was wrong with the truck, for it started itself up and smashed into a Jaguar that sat in the yard. He disconnected the battery so that it couldn't start itself again. The garage couldn't figure out what was wrong, so I drove it home and just kept disconnecting the battery. I never did figure out what was wrong with that truck.

So we are on the road doing burritos with the old school bus, and, man, it was so hot. We just had come from a Country Music Festival in Brooks. When my boy and his friend were about twelve years old, they traveled with us. One time when we were all unloading watermelons, our friend dropped one. His stepfather, who was also our boss, went crazy on him and made him stay in a hot tent for the whole day in the full sun. It was thirty degrees Celsius, which was very hot. Man, that was so cruel and no one could say anything that could save the young man from that heat.

So off to the first Edmonton Musical festival. I would stand by the seat and drive the old bus with the choke on because it was a straight road for miles. Our young friend said that he need to go to the washroom and couldn't hold it anymore. So I opened the bus door while he took a piss out of the door. So here we were going down the freeway at fifty miles an hour and this kid was pissing out the front side entrance door of the bus. That was when we heard the scream and shout, "Who just pissed on me?"

Good thing the reporter didn't ask me what was on my mind. What was really on my mind was that she was talking to a physiologist and some doctors over in Victoria about some nutcase on Salt Spring Island with his feet embedded in concrete. She told me that some physiologist wanted to come over and have a talk with me on the fourth day.

My mind was on fire, the zephyrs in my head fanned the coals of fright deep into the night. Thoughts flickered, never settling on one idea because there was just too many to cope with. One of the main thoughts that I had was what to do with the job that was offered to me. Should I sign a contract to be part of the Chaplaincy Act for Correction Canada? The Grand Mother always called regional headquarters the "big house." I had to quit that other job, after all, in order to follow my dream, and I got that old woman out of a big jam. No one knows really what would have happened if those papers for the society were not filed and brought up to date. Then there was that huge mystery of who scratched out those three top directors, which included the president of the society and the Grand Mother. There were many of us who had our suspicions as to why someone would do that. If someone were to take control of the society, they could have made millions of dollars from derailing the nonprofit group. In short, I quit and sat there thinking to myself, *Now what?*

It was the teachings that I had received that the corrections system wanted me to share. It was the main reason that they offered me tobacco when they gave me the opportunity of holding a contract with the Correction Service of Canada. My problem was, how would I do this if I decided to take the offer? It was selling the teachings because I would be getting a paycheck. I asked for the advice of an elder who had been around the block a few times.

He said, "Your people need help on the inside. They have been abandoned over the years, and they did offer you tobacco when they asked you to take the position." I also mentioned about how I was taught about the sweat lodge, to only build it for a specific ceremony and then burn it afterward. However, they never did that on the inside. He said, "Well, you can put special prayers out when you build the lodge." I sat there mulling over all these thoughts in my mind.

I could build a lodge for each season when we do our prayers for the lodge. Then at the start of a new season, I could burn the old one and go get new willows to build a new one for that season. That would mean building four lodges a year, I realized, as my mind was weighed down with thoughts of life. We never knew where we were going to go after the mountain. I still had the mountain dream in my head even though my dream of living in the past was gone by a stroke of a pen.

We were absolutely broke. I could just feel and see people's thoughts about me. They thought I was crazy man who could have made a lot of money if I would have just signed the rezoning papers. No wonder they wanted a physiologist to come and talk to me. Well, for probably more reasons than just the feet that needed circulation. All around me was my labor of love, everywhere I laid my eyes. I saw splotches of sweat that had dripped from my brow as I lifted the beams into place. It was twenty years later that I sat here and wrote this part. I had tried many times to finish my story but was never able to owing to my emotion.

THE LOCALS IN YUKON

I had gone to do work with one of the local bands in the Yukon, and for years they wanted me to have a piece of land. A few years ago, I decided to pursue this offer after we got the approval from the band's land department to have a piece of land. We got the OK from everyone involved, so we sent the papers to the Yukon government. After some time, they sent back a bunch of papers saying everything was fine. We needed $3,500 for a nonrefundable deposit on the land. This piece of land would be like having our mountain back. It sat high on the base of a mountain, covered with a large spruce tree forest and looked all over the Petty Mountain Range. It was breathtaking and faced due south with a lake right below. It felt like God's country personified.

Finally, the letter came from the Yukon government that stated all the terms of the for-sale agreement. After receiving this letter, I wrote a letter stating that we couldn't survey and put stakes in the earth and to consider this matter closed once and for all. Everyone up there said that if we had signed, the twenty-acre piece of land would have been ours. It would be like putting $80,000 in the bank. I'm not a perfect human being, and I have done a lot of stupid things in my day, but I will never subdivide Mother Earth from her wholeness.

When the final letter came and said this was our last chance, I said, "OK, let's do this." We would have been crazy not to because we had no land or house at that time. As the papers started coming again from the government, I was up in the Yukon doing the ceremony and made a mark where the boundaries were that a surveying company could use when they surveyed the said lands. I had three survey outfits, and any one of them was more than willing to do the job. When it came right down to paying the final check to the company we picked, after giving them a deposit I said I couldn't do it anymore. This was after we had put about $5,000 into it, and there would be no return on the funds.

Done over with never want to hear from you again about this subject Mr. Yukon Government, I had made my decision. At this point and much earlier, Kimi had told me it was my decision. I kicked myself many times over that decision. Over the years, I kept going up to the Yukon when I was invited to do some ceremonies, and the brothers always said just move onto the land.

When I went up to the Yukon last year to help save the historic foot bridge at Ross River, right after coming back from being invited to Peru to do a ceremony, my brothers said that I've got to move onto my land and that it was just sitting there waiting for me. It has sat there for the last twelve years or so. All I could think about was karma. Was this what it was all about? Saying no to survey stakes and just being able to move onto a piece of Mother Earth that was away in the middle of nowhere and had no survey stakes hammered into her soil of erosion from the past? So if you were to ask me today or tomorrow if it was worth it. I would say, yes, it was worth it, 100 percent. All you need is no fear, 100 percent faith, forgiveness, and no judgment. All my relations.

Keep an eye and ear open for my next book ! Inside Out ! it's about working inside the fence with our Native Brothers and Sisters as a Native Elder, some who have been ignored by society and locked away for their whole life. Thanks for reading my book, I enjoy sharing my life with you.

54482041R00136

Made in the USA
Charleston, SC
04 April 2016